D1097393

E-BOOK YOUR
TICKET TO
FREEDOM

*How Anyone Can Write an Ebook That
Sells, Earn a Passive Income, and
Escape the 9-5 Forever.*

BY NICHOLAS WOODS

NICHOLAS WOODS

SPECIAL BONUS!

Want this book for Free?

Get FREE, unlimited access to it and all of our new books by joining our community!

SCAN WITH YOUR CAMERA TO JOIN!

TABLE OF CONTENTS

INTRODUCTION

Anyone who has spent time on the internet will have noticed the incredible Ebook industry. All around the world, thousands of people are making fortunes writing and selling Ebooks. If you're reading this, it's probably because you'd like to join their ranks. You want to earn passive income selling Ebooks and live the life of a writer and entrepreneur.

But Where do you Start?
Writing a book can be a daunting task. It's probably one of the hardest things you'll ever do. Very few people consider themselves writers. Most of us never have to write anything in our day-to-day lives. Maybe you did some writing in high school or college, but this isn't nearly the same as writing a book. You have to realize that it is a skill like any other. If you're willing to put in time and effort, it's more than possible to master this skill. Think back to any new skill you've gained. There was an initial period where you understood nothing, but over time - and with practice - your skills gradually improved, and you passed out of this

state. Writing works precisely the same way. If you work on this, you will improve. It's almost guaranteed.

What also makes the process simpler is having a system. You need a guide or series of steps to follow. This is what this book is going to give you. By the time we're done, you'll have a clear road map that will take you from start to finish. With this road map, your book will be completed in no time at all. Not only that, you'll have written something that people actually want to buy. You're going to learn all the insider tips for success. How to decide what type of book to write, as well as the marketing tricks for selling your books more effectively, plus how to do data research to find a profitable niche suited to you. I'm also going to show you how to get someone to ghostwrite your book if that's the path you want to take.

Ultimately, it's not just the writing that's important. You don't have to be Shakespeare to make money with Ebooks. What's infinitely more important is the content of your book. What makes a book good isn't just the quality of the writing. No, a book is good when people feel they have received value from it and when you help them achieve the specific goal your book promises to deliver. And with this guide, that's exactly what you're going to learn how to do. You will see how using the correct keywords and Amazon SEO will make your book as profitable as possible, how you can have multiple income streams from writing only 1 or 2 books, and how to automate 90% of the work.

The people who make money from Ebooks are ordinary people, just like you and me. There's nothing special about them. Think about the celebrities who use ghostwriters. These people have no writing skills at all, and yet they can make millions from their books. The bottom line is that anyone can do this once they know the skills and tricks involved.

Promise

I want to make a promise to you right now. By the end of this book, you will have a deep understanding of what it takes to write a book of value and all the steps involved. You will have the knowledge and skills necessary to research your niche and make your book as profitable as possible. You will know how to write, market, and profit from your Ebook – and you will be able to do it as efficiently as possible.

Before I end this introduction, I want to give you a warning. It's critically important that you understand that Ebook writing is a type of gold rush. And like any gold rush, there's a good chance that the money will one day run out. Every day, tech companies become more draconian. There's no telling how long this industry will last or what the future holds for Ebooks. Now, I'm not telling you this to sound negative, but you should realize that time is of the essence. You need to take action and get started on this project. You should understand that your opportunities for profiting with Ebooks are almost unlimited. Much of the market is still untapped.

The world is constantly changing, which means new opportunities are continually being created (think of how COVID-19 has changed the world and how you could profit from this situation). Also, realize that for every good book written, there are dozens of bad ones. Couldn't you do better? You probably could, and the rewards for putting in the time and effort are almost infinite. Imagine what life would be like if you were a successful Ebook writer. Imagine never having to get up and work for someone else again, traveling the world and doing what you want when you want… and having enough money to do it. It may sound like a cliché, but you only live once. It's up to you to make the most of this life.

This might sound like a fantasy, but it can become a reality. That being said, it will only happen if you're willing to take action and dive into the deep end. Be prepared, but don't overprepare! You learn along the way, just like when someone is thrown into the deep end of a swimming pool. They now have no choice but to swim or figure out how. I speak in detail about this in chapter 8, why often it's better to move before you are ready in life. And if you make an effort, it can happen faster than you ever thought possible. There's no reason you shouldn't be able to write, upload, and sell the first copy of your Ebook within 30 days from now. If you repeat that process over a 6-month period and have multiple books selling, there is every chance you will make a passive income more significant than what a regular job pays. Better still, you could soon be an automated Ebook business owner and never have to work for someone else again. While this may sound impossible right now, the skills and tools you're about to learn about can make it a reality. I've done it, and so have thousands of other people.

I want you to utilize this book and navigate through it however you like. Skip ahead to different chapters, and come back. For example, if you already have a book idea but need to come up with a good title, skip to chapter 6. If you just want to start writing, you can go to chapters 7 and 8. Don't get too bogged down reading and worrying about things like 'data research' and 'funnels' just yet. What separates this book from others on this topic is the tips and guidelines on the **actual writing** of books and the art of storytelling. So many other books have all the information on publishing and marketing your book but not nearly enough tips on actually writing it and how best to go about it. I also have an entire bonus chapter on 'The Art of Copywriting,' which could be a book in itself. This book has everything you need. Now, let's get started!

CHAPTER 1

Why You Should Definitely Write a Book

You have a unique perspective on something. *"What if I just work in a boring office job or Carphone Warehouse?"* you say. Well, it's still a unique perspective on something. It's still recollections, it's still experiences. Just like Steve Carell in the sitcom "The Office" making something that seems so mundane and boring be something so human and brilliant. Maybe you have been doing something for 5, 10, or 15 years that you love doing as a hobby. Whether it's playing an instrument, doing open mics for comedy, writing poetry, bird-watching, playing a sport, or running yoga classes, whatever it is, it could be anything. You have specialist knowledge in something, and someone out there wants to know about it. You can pass on that information and speak about the mistakes you made, the lessons you learned, and your experiences. The old cliché of *'everyone has a book inside them'* is true. It's there inside you, but if it's not written down, it doesn't exist. When you eventually leave this world and return to ashes, if it's not written down, if it's not online, if it's not in a library or on paperback or hardback, it doesn't exist. All those ideas, dreams, experiences, and unique perspectives are gone forever.

Writing is Therapeutic

Writing can also be very therapeutic. Reliving experiences, even if bad, can often be extremely therapeutic and help deal with situations and release anxiety. If it's about pleasant past experiences, then all the better. Victor E. Frankl is a holocaust survivor who wrote accounts of his horrific experiences in a Nazi concentration camp in Auschwitz, Poland, during World War 2 in the mid-1900s. While the details in his book *'Mans Search for Meaning'* were shocking, it turned out to be a therapeutic process for Frankl. He developed a new philosophy called *'Logotherapy'* from writing these accounts and surviving these horrific experiences. This philosophy is based on how having meaning in life, no matter how small or minute, can help you overcome any circumstance or obstacle you face in life. His book has inspired millions of people across the world, and his philosophy is still helping people to this day. It's a must-read, and I advise anyone who hasn't read it to do so. Nobody would have known the finer details of what he went through and how he was able to survive. I realize this is an extreme example, but if you have been through something difficult in your life, no matter how big or small, that is something to be proud of. On the flip side, if you have achieved something in your life that you are proud of, no matter how big or small, documenting it will also help someone. So, I encourage you to do it, to write the book you've always wanted to. Not just for the potential of earning an income but also for the therapeutic aspect of it.

Writing is a Muscle

Writing is a muscle. It's a skill. It's a habit. And it can be bloody painful. Nobody feels like sitting down and writing, not even the best writers in the world. Especially not at the beginning. If you wait to feel like writing, you'll be waiting forever. But here is the disclaimer. Once you start writing and you're on to day 10 or 15 of a 30-day promise, you will want to keep going. It's immersive. It's quiet. It's a wonderfully selfish pursuit with something to show for it in the end. As I mentioned, it's therapy. And when the book is finished, you feel a bit of a loss. Like when you finish watching a TV series that you were deeply invested in. Humans love working towards a goal, a project. And it's never about the result - it's the journey that is the most enjoyable part. While writing your first book, you may say to yourself, *'when this is over, I will never write again.'* But as soon as you finish, you will be thinking about the next project, which could very well be another book.

To write yourself, you need to read. Not crazy amounts of reading, but regular reading a few times a week. Good writers are good readers. Through reading, you understand narrative arcs and the layout of books. The more you read, the more you will get inspiration for ideas. Writing is the ideal pursuit, especially for an introverted person. It can be pursued by anybody, introverted or extroverted. As an ex-academic and former school teacher, I prefer nonfiction—textbook type, guides, the arts of philosophies, etc. I was a practical subject school teacher. I like to crystallize ideas, make things clear in my mind, and create simple, practical steps with none of the excess theory and fluff that many books have today.

This part of the book is to plant the seed of confidence in your subconscious mind that - yes, you can write a book. It's a win-win because you can potentially make a passive income. And if not, it is still a therapeutic process. Writing is total solitude. Its flow-state. It's meditation. It's a descent into the inner world of oneself. But it also can put you in your head, into the over-analytical thinking mind. So, it's essential to get outside every couple of hours and get into the fresh air of nature. Balance is key. It will boost your creativity. Chapter 10 on overcoming writer's block goes into more detail on this.

CHAPTER 2

Self-Publishing, What Is It?

How do you Publish?

You may be wondering how Ebooks are published. How do you actually get your book online? The answer is that there are almost unlimited ways to publish your Ebook. That being said, the most common publishing method is through KDP (Kindle Direct Publishing). There are many advantages to using this platform. The biggest is that it gives you access to the millions of people who buy from this website. Amazon is almost like a gigantic shopping center that is visited by millions of people on a daily basis.

What's also great about Amazon is the question of credibility. The reason why you want to publish on this platform is because of trust. People know, like, and trust the Amazon brand. They have no problem buying from this site, which may be a problem on other platforms.

What's also great about Amazon is that it gives you the option to have your books produced as paperbacks. Second to Amazon is Lulu. This is another site that publishes paperback/hardback copies of books. Lulu is a print-on-demand service. What this means is that copies of your book are printed as they are ordered and are shipped directly to the buyer. Yet another option is audiobooks. You can upload your book as an audiobook onto Amazon Audible by having it narrated by a professional.

Aside from this, there are dozens of ways to publish Ebooks for free. In the chapters to come, we will talk about all the platforms where you can upload your books. Ultimately, you want to upload your books onto as many platforms as possible. This is the secret to generating multiple streams of revenue from each book.

How much can you Earn?

So how much can you earn from Ebooks? This is the million-dollar question, and the answer is that there is no simple answer. The amount of money you make depends on dozens of factors. These include the price point of your Ebooks, how many copies you sell, and, most importantly, the quality of your product. How much you make also depends on how much effort you're willing to put in.

Publishing Ebooks is the same as any other business.

The harder you work, the more money you'll make. That being said, it's more than possible to make between $200-$2000 per month. This is highly doable for anyone, even beginners. You can make this money by selling only 20-30 copies monthly. Also, consider this: even if you only make $200 per month, that income is passive and automated. Once you've written the book, much of the hard work is over. From there on out, you will be making passive income.

On the other hand, as we've said, the more work you put into the marketing side of things, the more you will make. And the sky's the limit if you publish 3, 4, or even 10 + books. This is especially true if you research popular genres and niches and target markets with high demand and low competition. Do this, and it's more than possible to earn $2000 or more per month.

There are self-publishers out there now making six figures a year from Ebooks. Now, you don't want to get ahead of yourself, and that type of income is a long way down the line, but it is possible to make this amount of money. There is so much profit to be made because you are *self-publishing*. With traditional publishing, you'd be lucky to receive even 10% of the book's cover price. Publishers take the lion's share, and authors receive a pittance. This is just one of the many reasons traditional publishing is dying.

How is it Automated?

There's a lot of talk about automation for Ebook publishing, but what does this mean? Essentially, once the book is written, your work is done. There is no physical work required to sell it. For example, you upload your book to Amazon, the buyer adds it to the cart, and a month later, the money is in your bank account. Yes, you must market and advertise your book correctly, but we will touch on this later.

What type of books can you write?
In chapter 3, we'll talk more about the types of books you can write. For now, you need to understand that you can write anything. That being said, the most important thing is that you need to create a book for which there is a market. If you write books that no one wants to read, you're unlikely to make much money. This is why it's essential to combine writing what you are passionate about with finding a market for that niche. You can tailor your book toward a better target market with simple changes to titles and subtitles.

How long does the book need to be?
Not to sound redundant, but there is no straightforward answer to this question. It's like asking 'how long is a piece of string? What's important is that the reader feels they have derived value from the book. That your book has answered their question, helped them solve a problem, or taught them some valuable skill. For example, let's say you write a healthy diet book. What matters isn't the length of the book. No, what matters is that the reader can maintain a healthy diet by using the information in your book. Some of the most successful books have been less than 10,000

words. The length of your book will also depend on the genre. Fiction books vary in size, while nonfiction books are generally shorter. I believe the magic mark for Ebooks is between 25-35000 words. But quality and value are the most critical elements of your book.

How do you market your book without a following?
Marketing is one of the most important aspects of being an Ebook entrepreneur. As mentioned earlier, the more work you put into marketing your books, the more money you'll make. Conversely, if you don't put any work into selling your products, you won't maximize your earnings. Now, don't let this put you off. What's great about being an Ebook publisher is that the internet gives you almost unlimited ways to market your books. For example, social media is the most obvious way to sell Ebooks. Social media platforms give you enormous reach and scope for marketing your books. Billions of people use these sites, which means you have thousands of potential customers.

Another way is through paid advertising. Once again, the internet provides limitless ways to advertise your Ebooks (and do it cheaply). For example, Amazon and Facebook ads are cheap, simple, and easy to set up. When done right, you can sell hundreds of books per month with these ads.

SEO
One of the most popular ways to promote any product these days is through SEO. This acronym stands for **S**earch **E**ngine **O**ptimization, and it's essentially the art

and methods of getting websites and products to the top of the search results. With the right SEO, you can push your books to the top of the search results and get thousands of visitors to your website or Amazon listing. This is a highly complex subject, and we'll discuss it in more detail later. But basically, it involves research and finding a niche in a market with high demand and low competition. It is possible to sell books through SEO alone.

Funnels

Something else you need to understand about marketing is the concept of funnels (or sales funnel, as they are also known). A funnel is a marketing concept where you provide content, drive visitors to that content, capture their details and then follow up with those visitors. So, let's say you're an expert in real estate or physical training. In this case, you could create content on a platform like YouTube, Facebook, or TikTok. Perhaps you'll make videos where you talk about how to lose weight, build muscle, or get into shape. Maybe you'll talk about how to make money in real estate. Or you may get cool video edits made with voiceovers on a freelance website if you are not comfortable in front of the camera. Over time people will begin to follow you, sharing and liking your posts. This will take time, and you're looking at about six months to build up a following, depending on how active you are (although with TikTok, it could be far sooner). Once you've amassed an audience and people are enjoying your content, you'll start to send these people to your website (alternatively, you could send them to your Amazon or Lulu page).

Now, a lot of this might sound complicated or beyond your reach right now, but don't worry. You don't *have to* create a social media profile or a website. Your book will begin to generate sales by itself with good SEO and some Amazon ads. And if you do decide to create a website, you can always hire a freelancer to build the website for you. There are hundreds of quality freelancers in places like Upwork or Fiverr. These people can be hired at a reasonable price and can be relied upon to provide quality results. You don't have to feel overwhelmed by this. Even if you have no technical skills or don't understand something, it doesn't mean you have to give up. Also, remember that this is the end stage of the Ebook business, the first step is writing your book, and then you can worry about the marketing.

What is Ghostwriting?

Ghostwriting is when you pay someone to write a book for you. In this case, your name will be attached to the book as the author. Not only that, any money you receive from the book sales will be entirely yours. An excellent example of ghostwriting is celebrity biographies. Another good example is biographies of sportspeople which you always see in bookstores. Almost every successful sportsperson has a biography. And believe me, 99% of the athletes didn't write those books.

Yet another example is books written by politicians. You may have noticed that most politicians (especially in

America if they are running for office) have a book. Ghostwriters create the overwhelming majority of these books.

Whether you decide to use a ghostwriter depends on various factors, the most significant one being money. Writing a book yourself costs nothing except time. On the other hand, you need money to hire a ghostwriter. That being said, it's not as expensive as you might think, and it's possible to find talented freelancers if you look hard enough. Another advantage of ghostwriters is that they can make the process more efficient. Writing books is hard work and time-consuming. You can focus on other things by hiring someone else to do the hard work, like marketing your books. You could hire multiple writers to create a line of books and launch your Ebook empire in no time at all. This is a good option for people who are not yet confident in their writing skills. Instead of doing the writing, you can focus on things like market research, editing the final product, or designing covers for your books.

Using a ghostwriter still means you'll have to put in work. It's not as simple as telling your writer that you want a book written on, let's say, intermittent fasting. Doing this will only lead to failure, and it's not recommended. You cannot simply hand over responsibility to a stranger and expect them to do a good job. Another thing you have to realize is that if you do things this way, the book will be written from the ghostwriter's perspective, and maybe that's something you'd like to avoid.

The bottom line is that, even if you use a ghostwriter, you still have to give them a detailed outline. It's imperative that you take time to create things like your table of contents, the topics you want written about, and the overall direction of the book. Putting effort into this outline will boost your chances of a high-quality book that will sell. In chapter 12, we will be going into more detail on this.

CHAPTER 3

Types of Books You Can Start Writing About Today

So, what are you going to write about? Anyone who has purchased this book probably did so because **a)** you wanted to create a stream of income selling Ebooks or **b)** you have a specific idea for a book and need help writing and publishing it. If you're in the first category, your most pressing problem is coming up with an idea for your Ebook. This is a lot easier than it might seem. When writing an Ebook, there are only two main types. Fiction and nonfiction.

NONFICTION BOOKS

Most Ebooks are nonfiction. Of these books, the most popular Ebooks can be loosely described as "how-to guides." These are books that teach or show you how to do something.

1. Topic-Based Guides to Certain Ideas

This category can include many different things. It often covers guides relating to specific psychological, mindset, or self-help topics. Speaking of self-help, this is an enormously popular category when it comes to Ebooks. It's probably the most popular category in the world. There are hundreds and hundreds of self-help Ebooks covering a dazzling variety of topics.

There are books on how to meditate, manage your time more effectively, achieve your goals, get a better job, manage your money, improve your relationships, think better, write better, speak in public, or even overcome addiction problems. The list is almost limitless, and if you're looking for an Ebook topic, consider finding a unique niche in the self-help category.

You also have more esoteric topics in this genre. For example, there are Ebooks on things like numerology, astrology/star signs, developing your psychic intuition, the law of attraction, contacting angels, delving into past lives, and so on. These could be categorized as "spiritual" Ebooks, and if you're interested in this stuff, you might want to write about it.

Something else that's interesting is the religious category. If you're religious, you can write something related to that. No matter what religion or faith you subscribe to, there's probably an Ebook waiting to be written.

2. Personal Stories / Narrative Nonfiction / Inspirational Stories

Do you have a personal story you'd like to share with the world? There's no reason you shouldn't write about it, especially if it's something other people might also experience or go through in their lives. There are dozens of examples in this category.

You may be an abuse survivor. Perhaps you overcame some horrifying experience or challenge in life. There is every chance someone else has gone through a similar experience and will take massive value from your story. You can take real pride in working on this type of book. Something that's also popular is alcohol and addiction memoirs. You may even want to write a true-crime story or biography of some obscure person. While the market for these types of books may be smaller than others, they are still worth writing about, especially if your story is unique.

Maybe you went on a crazy adventure on a backpacking trip across South America or Europe and discovered unique towns and villages off the beaten track. There really is no limit to the type of personal stories you can write about.

3. Instructional Books and Guides

As I've said, instructional and "how-to guides" are by far

the most popular Ebooks. This category can also be broken down into dozens of different subcategories. Something that might help you is thinking in terms of health, wealth, and relationships. The most popular how-to guides usually have something to do with these topics.

For example, the health category would include books on how to lose weight, build muscle, get six-pack abs, do yoga and pilates, go rock climbing, or finish a marathon. This category also includes books on specific health problems. Something extremely popular right now is how-to guides relating to type 2 diabetes. Next, you have the wealth category. This might include anything which shows you how to make or save money. For example, something that's always popular is 'guides to making money with stocks and financial investments. The wealth category also includes ways to develop a side hustle, make money online, or earn money with real estate investing.

You also have the relationship category. This covers anything related to relationships and romantic partners. For example, "how to get a girlfriend" Ebooks are still immensely popular, as are books about finding the man of your dreams and so on. Then you have Ebooks on how to stop your divorce or develop a deeper connection with your spouse and children. Finally, you have what could loosely be referred to as the "improve your love life" niche. This covers various topics but basically boils down to showing people how to improve their sex life. You could explore this niche if you cannot think of anything else to write about.

Now, you don't necessarily have to write a book about

health, wealth, or relationships. All I am saying is that these are the most popular books, and it helps to write something in this category. That said, you can pretty much write on anything under the sun. For example, anything related to cookery for food usually does well if the quality is there.

You could also write about sports. Maybe you can share tips on how to improve your golf game, fly fishing, or skateboarding. Another popular niche is the pet niche. There are literally dozens of different animals for which you can write guides. You could create an Ebook related to the care and feeding of birds, bearded dragons, cats, dogs, guinea pigs, horses, you name it!

4. Academic Textbooks & Manuals, Guides to Technology

If you're an educator, teacher, or professor, you might like to write a textbook. This is also an excellent choice for engineers or those who work in the IT industry. It's harder to give an example of these types of books. But if you're someone who works in the educational or technology field, then you may already have an idea for a book. Kid's educational books are also very popular.

5. Turn Your Blog/Podcast/Videos into a Book

If you're a content creator, you may already have enough material for a book. The way you do this is by recycling or repurposing old content. For example, you could turn your blog posts, podcasts, or videos into Ebooks. This is actually a great idea because it allows you to save vast amounts of time. Instead of wasting your time creating new content, you simply rework content you have already created.

FICTION BOOKS

If you don't want to write nonfiction books, then there's always fiction. Before we get started on this, I want to warn you. If you're serious about making money with Ebooks, then you're advised against creating works of literature. It might sound harsh, but the market for novels is almost non-existent, especially on the internet. If you write fiction books, it's best to stick to what's known as genre fiction.

This concept encompasses fiction books that fit into certain predetermined categories. The best example of this is romance novels. Other forms of genre fiction include science fiction / fantasy / horror, and also detective novels / thrillers / adventure. What's great about writing these Ebooks is that you can still make them profitable. Overall, genre fiction sells very well.

The 50 Shades of Grey series is probably the most famous example. Did you know this series started life as an Ebook? Most people don't. Despite these humble beginnings, this series has now sold over 15 million copies and made over $100 million for the author E. L. James. If this isn't a testament to the incredible power of Ebooks, then I don't know what is. It's also an example of what's possible if you put in the effort. Now, you're unlikely to have this type of success, but it's perfectly realistic to earn $100, $500 even $1000 per month with these Ebooks.

The bottom line is that some of the world's most

successful novelists write genre fiction. Authors like Nora Roberts (romance), Stephen King (horror), and James Patterson (thrillers) sell books by the thousands and are multi-millionaires. There's no reason you shouldn't be able to replicate their success, at least to a lesser extent, with Ebooks. With platforms like Amazon and devices like Kindle, this is a lot easier than it seems. Did you know Amazon has sold over 90 million Kindle devices? How many of these people are potential customers for your novels?

Do Your Research

The best advice I can give you when trying to figure out what type of book you want to write is to familiarize yourself with what's already available. You need to do your research. Start by visiting local bookshops. Visit as many as you can.

Walk around and look at what's on the shelves. Start with the nonfiction sections and look at what's available. What types of books do you see in the psychology section, the self-help section, the health and wellness section, the spirituality section, and the business section?   Next, look through the fiction areas. Pay special attention to the fiction genre we spoke about previously. Go through the romance, thriller, and science fiction/fantasy sections. Which authors are famous, and what are their books about? Could you do better, and if so, what would you write about? Take as much time as you want and look through as many books as you can. Doing this will give you an idea of what's possible and should help to inspire you.

After this, visit sites like Amazon and Lulu. Do the same thing. Have a look at what's available and what people seem to buy. Click through every category and see what the system shows you. You can also enter keywords in the search bar. For example, if you're thinking of writing a real estate Ebook, enter keywords related to this niche and see what comes up.

This research should be expanded onto the internet as a whole. You need to become observant and pay attention to what's happening online. It's a good idea to take notes on this. Whenever you stumble upon an Ebook that interests you, make a note of it. Think about the genre the book fits into, what made it successful, and how you could do it differently and better. Read good and bad reviews on books you are interested in writing.

Once you've done that, try to brainstorm ideas. On a piece of paper, jot down 5 to 10 ideas you have for your book. Think of a unique skill set you may have gained over the years or a unique experience you have that you can share with the world. Think of ways you can help people or some type of benefit you could share with them. Consider what kind of book you want to write, what interests you, and what you would ideally like to write about.

CHAPTER 4

Data Research and SEO Tricks Every Writer Needs to Know

The success of your Ebook will often come down to how well you research the market. It's critical that you find a niche where there is little competition but, at the same time, enough of an audience for you to turn a profit. It would be best if you found a niche with high demand and low competition on the Amazon kindle store. Doing this will significantly boost your chances of success.

As I've said, your most powerful research tool is Amazon. By going through the Amazon kindle store, you'll be able to figure out what's popular and see what types of books are in demand. The Amazon search function makes this easy. It gives you the option to filter searches by best sellers. You can look through the different categories to see which are the most popular and in great demand. You should also pay attention to other keywords that pop up as suggestions in the search bar. These suggestions are a way of gauging what other people are also searching for. For example, if you type in 'yoga,' the suggestions that may pop up are 'yoga for beginners, 'yoga for weight loss, 'yoga for back pain, and so on. Once you type in a keyword or search terms as it is called sometimes, the top 20 books that appear are the best-selling books for that keyword in order. All of this is essentially SEO.

In case you don't know, this is basically how Google works. People type in keywords, and pages containing those keywords appear in the search results. Your job is to determine which keywords people are entering and create a book based on those keywords. For example, one of the most common topics is weight loss. When looking for books about weight loss, people will type in keywords like "fast weight loss," "simple weight loss," or "best weight loss." If you want to appear in the Amazon search results, you need to insert these keywords into your book title.

When you search for a keyword, you can also check the BSR of each of the first books that appear. **BSR** is an acronym for **B**est **S**ellers **R**anking. You can then type that ranking into a BSR calculator (free online tool), which will estimate how many sales that book is making per month.

KDSPY

Simply put, KDSPY is the number one tool (along with publisher rocket) every writer and self-publisher should have. It's an easy-to-use chrome extension for your laptop or computer. KDSPY will show you all the data for the top 20 best sellers' books available for whatever keyword you search in the amazon search bar and the BSR of each book. From there, it also gives you the average BSR of those books. If the average is around 200,000 or below, you have established that this keyword has high demand and will be profitable. You can do this data research with as many keywords as you like and find what is in high demand. And if the search results are 9000 or below for that keyword, then you have also found out that this keyword is in medium to low demand. This is precisely what you're looking for. High demand, low competition. It will also tell you how many monthly sales are made and how much revenue each book makes.

Similar tools and software are available that do the same thing, but most require a monthly subscription that adds up over time. KDSPY is a one-time payment. It's been the best investment I've made in my writing publishing journey. I use it almost every day. A simple adjustment of a keyword or subtitle can put the same book you have written into a niche where there is high demand, and so you have the potential to get far more sales and revenue.

Play around with this tool, and you will soon be able to use it with ease. A little trick is when looking at the average BSR, x off a couple of outliers with a really high BSR and will bring the average down to a lower, more realistic number which is more accurate.

KDSPY link:

(I have Shortened the KDSPY download link below for you to easily type into your computer.)

tinyurl.com/KDSPYlink

Here is a KDSPY blog post if you would like to know more:

tinyurl.com/kdspyblog

***

Amazon Reviews (3-Star)

Another powerful research tool is Amazon reviews. When doing the data research for your book, look through the best-selling books in that niche. From there, look through the 3-star reviews of those books. These tend to be the most honest. The customer doesn't have an agenda against the book, nor do they love it. You will see the pros and cons of the book and a reoccurring point on something about the book that was lacking or missing. This will help you determine what mistakes those authors made and what they may have done right.

To find a good niche in the market, you will have to do this type of data research and learn about SEO and keywords. There are entire books written about keywords and SEO alone. Of course, it's important to find a topic that interests you and you know about it or have experience with it.

Once you can figure out if that area has relatively low competition and relatively high demand, you can then think about writing your book. Just note that there are no rules. You can write any book that you want, but this will help make your book more profitable. You could title and or subtitle a book in such a way that it falls into a category with better demand and lower competition. At the end of the day, it's going to be about the quality of the work produced.

CHAPTER 5

Who is Your Book For? - Discovering Your Target Audience

A big part of your success or failure will depend on finding the right target audience. You need to find a market of rabid and hungry buyers. You need a group of people who are seeking to solve their problems. An excellent example is people who want to lose weight and get fit. These people will often buy dozens of diet books, always hoping to find some type of miracle weight loss cure. Of course, it always boils down to hard work, but keep it in mind. What your market is really buying is the promise of a new beginning.

A transformation that will improve their lives and make them feel happier in their own skin.

Think of it like this: what if I said you could completely transform your body and do it with just a few tweaks to your diet and routine? That I had a brand-new weight-loss method that has already worked for thousands of people? And this secret is contained within the pages of my book… and… all you have to do is buy the book, and your life will be transformed. This is what you're really selling to people.

Also, be aware that categories like 'weight loss and 'self-help are massively saturated, so it's best to find niches within them. For example, a diet book for post-pregnancy weight loss or a meditation book for beginners. These are niches within those categories targeting a more specific audience.

As mentioned previously, you need to visit the bookstore. When you do this, pay particular attention to the books in the self-help section. What you may notice about these books is that they all have a promise behind them. These books promise you some kind of benefit. Whether that's losing weight, having a better relationship, or improving your time management. The bottom line is that you need to find a group of people with some kind of problem. You then have to help them escape that problem and enter a new reality. Ultimately, you want to answer a burning question that is on their mind or help them figure out a solution to a problem they are currently struggling with.

Here are some questions to ask yourself when trying to figure out your target market:

- What is your market struggling with right now?
- What keeps them up at night, staring at the ceiling in a cold sweat?
- What benefits does your market most desperately crave?
- Do they want to lose weight, solve a specific health problem, or earn more money?
- What specific promise are you making in your book?
- How will reading your book transform, change, or alter their life?
- How specific can you make your target market?

This last point is particularly important. You want to make your target market specific and narrow. Avoid writing something general. For example, don't write a book about *stress management*. Instead, write something like, "*how to become stress-free in two weeks.*" The more specific you can be, the better. You want to write a book that answers the *exact* question your market is asking. Remember, your market is buying the book to answer a question or solve their problem.

Joining the Conversation in Their Head

Ultimately, do your research and discover what's going on with your target market. This is often referred to as "joining the conversation in their head." Your target market thinks about its problems in a specific way. They talk to themselves using certain words and language. You want to use words and language which resonate with your market. The closer you can get to this, the better your book will be.

This is also why it helps to be part of the market you're writing about. You want to avoid writing about something entirely foreign to you. It is probably a bad idea if you're a young man writing a guide on raising children and you're not a father. On the other hand, if you're a personal trainer writing a fitness book, you'll already know your target market's wants, needs, fears, and desires.

Answering a specific question also means less competition. Another example is instead of writing a general weight-loss book, why not write a weight-loss book for people over 50? Doing things this way will boost your chances of success.

Groups

This brings us to our next point. Starting with demographics and psychographics is a great idea. Most people like to believe they are unique, but this usually isn't true. Similar groups of people have similar problems.

Think about things like gender, age, race, and location. These variables can be mixed up in a variety of ways. For example, women aged 25-40 who are newly married with small children. What type of problems could these people be facing? What kind of book could you write for them?

Something else to think about are psychographics. This word basically refers to particular traits or psychological attributes held by certain people. To put this more simply, it means that certain groups of people own a set of beliefs and may also have the same type of problems. An excellent example of this could be artists of all kinds. The most prominent problem artists face is the struggle to be creative. There are hundreds of books out there that promise to help with creativity and achieving *'Flow-State.'* Two best-selling examples are ***The War of Art*** by Stephen Pressfield and ***The Artist's Way*** by Julia Cameron.

Another common universal problem is the need to make friends. A book that answered this question was ***How to Win Friends & Influence People*** by Dale Carnegie. Then you have ***How to Stop Worrying and Start Living*** by the same author. Both books are world-famous and have sold millions of copies. The reason is that they answer ultra-specific questions many people want to know the answers to.

What you can also do is make a list of "famous" nonfiction books. These include books like ***Rich Dad Poor Dad, The 4-Hour Work Week, Think and Grow Rich, The Power of Now, The 7 Habits of Highly Effective People.*** These are some of the most well-known nonfiction books ever written.

Think about why these books were so successful:

- What specific questions do they answer?

- How do they promise to transform the reader's life?
- What benefits do they provide for the reader?
- How can you replicate their success?

An excellent exercise is reading books in the niche you're planning to write about. Think about what's common in these books. What do they tell you about the market, and how can you improve on what's already been done?

One of the biggest mistakes is putting the cart before the horse. Don't write your book until you know if there's a market for what you're writing. Doing this may result in a book no one wants to read. In order to make your book profitable, you need to understand that you're not just writing a book for yourself. Always, always keep the market in mind, and think about what they want, as well as what *you* want.

Therefore, data research is critical. You need to gauge if there's a market for your book before you write it. You can do this by browsing Amazon and also visiting your local bookshops.

Publisher Rocket

Publisher Rocket is one of the best research tools available when it comes to writing books. While KDSPY focuses more on the profitability of different niches and books, Publisher Rocket helps self-publishers and authors understand what readers *actually* want by giving more data on particular keywords that readers type in when searching for books. It's so good that traditional publishers are using it too. Again it's a one-time payment software that you install on your desktop. It's also easy to use and straightforward.

Here are certain things you can discover with Publisher Rocket:

- The phrases Amazon buyers are actually searching for and similar phrases to that keyword.
- The psychology of how readers choose to purchase books.
- How much money the readers are spending on specific niches and topics.
- How much money specific keywords and books are making per month
- How many searches are being made per month using the given keyword

With this knowledge, you can reverse-engineer potential titles, subtitles, descriptions, and so on with the confidence that they will do well on Amazon. (providing your book is also of decent quality)

The four main tools in PR are: **1.** Keyword Search Feature. **2.** Competition Analyzer Feature. **3.** Category Search Feature. **4.** AMS Keyword Search Feature

There are also simple tutorial videos included if you are a bit unsure. It really is a fun exercise to think up a potential keyword and then instantly search it on PR just to see how many searches per month that keyword gets and how profitable it may be.

Also, down the line, when creating Amazon ads once your book is live, you can use the recommended keywords that PR shows you that are similar to your own. These will help you generate more impressions and sales.

Publisher Rocket link:

(I have Shortened the Publisher Rocket download link below for you to easily type into your computer.)

tinyurl.com/procketlink

Here is a Publisher Rocket blog post if you would like to know more:

tinyurl.com/procketblog

***

While there are a vast number of tools and software recommended out there, KDSPY and PR are all you need to begin researching and writing the book you've always wanted to write.

CHAPTER 6

Deciding on a Great Title with Clever Use of Keywords

PLEASE NOTE: it is not essential to create your title before writing your book. Often the final title will come after the book has been written. If you have a rough idea of your title and just want to get started, you can move on to chapters 7 & 8 and come later to refine it. You will most likely come up with updated and improved title ideas as you write your book.

The title of your book is vitally important. This isn't something you should pull out of a hat once the book is written. You need to put time and effort into crafting a grand slam title. There are two reasons this is so important. The first is because your title needs to contain the right keywords, and the second is because your title will determine how well your book does.

By now, you should also understand the critical importance of keywords. Choosing the right keywords makes your book visible on Amazon and thus makes your book sell. This ultimately means that you must cleverly incorporate your chosen keywords into the title of your book. Again, **Publisher Rocket** is your go-to when it comes to all of this. It really is a game changer (download available in chapter 5).

Don't choose an abstract title, something you've become attached to, or something you think is clever or cute. You must select keywords that will help you come up in Amazon searches. To be profitable, the title will be dictated by the market and by what will do well on Amazon. Think in terms of results. If the person wants to lose weight, what keywords will they enter on Amazon?

Your title also needs to describe what the book is about clearly. You need to get your ideas across in only a few words. Something you should also definitely do is add a subtitle. This helps expand your title and is a great place to add more keywords. Subtitles are also a great place to use long-tail keywords. This will increase your search visibility and help you create a title that resonates with your market.

Something else to think about is the skill level of your market. Are you aiming for beginners, intermediates, or experts? Each of these groups has different needs, wants, desires, etc. Each of these groups will also give you access to a bigger or smaller market. There are always far more beginners than experts. Think about this when choosing a title for your book.

Breaking Down Titles - 3 examples:

One of the best examples of an impressive title is ***The 4-Hour Workweek***. The full title of this book is ***The 4-Hour Workweek: Escape the 9-5, Live Anywhere, and Join the New Rich.*** Think about how this title conveys the benefits of this book. Also, think about how it answers the questions and problems of the market. If we break this title down in greater detail, you'll see it contains four obvious benefits (each of which has tremendous emotional weight).

1) ***The 4-Hour Workweek***: the benefit that this book is going to show you is how to work only 4 hours a week. This is an incredible selling point and the reason the book did so well. Can you see how it solves the problem of people hating their jobs?

2) ***Escape the 9-5***: the benefit of quitting work and making money on the internet. That you no longer need to work at a job you hate.

3) ***Live Anywhere***: the benefit is that you can travel the world and live anywhere while still earning an income. This is a powerful emotional appeal. Many people dream of being able to travel the world. This book promises to show them how to do it.

4) ***Join the New Rich***: the idea that there is a new class of people, and you can become one of them. What's powerful about this final bit is that it creates the idea that you're missing out. That there's a group of people doing everything you already dream of. A group of people who have escaped their jobs. Can live anywhere they like and, most importantly, make money hand over fist while barely working. All you have to do to join this group of people is buy the book. This last bit of copywriting also sets up a powerful "us vs. them" dynamic.

Another great title is a book called ***The Life-Changing Magic of Tidying Up: The Japanese Art of Decluttering and Organizing***. Let's examine this title:

1. ***The Life-Changing Magic of Tidying Up***: this title promises to solve the problem of messy living circumstances and show you how to tidy up your life. More importantly, it promises that doing this is "Life-Changing" and "Magic."

2. ***The Japanese Art of Decluttering and Organizing***: the most important word in this subtitle is Japanese. It gives the title an exotic flavor and implies there is something that Japanese people know about tidying up that westerners don't. The promise is that by reading this book, you will learn these little-known Japanese tidying secrets. This word also works because Japan is

thought of as an orderly country. Then you have the words decluttering and organizing. Again, these are two benefits promised to the book's readers.

Our third example is an old book called **The Easy Way to Stop Smoking** by Allen Carr. This title is relatively straightforward but still powerful. It essentially promises that you can stop smoking quickly and do it with minimal effort. What makes this title effective is that most smokers perceive quitting as something incredibly difficult and also painful. You have to go through the unpleasant feeling of nicotine withdrawal. This book promises to help you avoid all that. It promises to show you a quick and easy way to quit without pain.

As you can see, these titles, while seemingly simple, have a lot going on behind the scenes. These are the things you need to do with your own titles. My advice is to start collecting titles. Write them down and think about the mechanics behind each title. What makes it work, what benefits are conveyed, and how can you adapt the title for your book?

Also, think about what makes your book unique and how you're going to get this across. In the above example, the word "Japanese" is what makes the title unique. What words can you use in your title to convey the idea of uniqueness?

Something else to note is that you need to think in terms of systems, methods, and techniques. What people really want is a step-by-step system for solving their problems. They want a secret method or technique for achieving their goals. All three of the previous title examples subtly convey the idea that you are going to be taught a system for achieving each book's promise.

By combining these tips, you should be able to come up with a decent title for your book. If you still need help, here is a step-by-step methodology for coming up with a name.

Choosing a Grand Slam Book Title:

1. Use Your Book

Many of the greatest titles were simply taken from the book itself. Look through your manuscript and see if there's a phrase that jumps out at you. Also, think about the fundamental idea behind your book. What is the promise you're making, and what's the best way to convey it to your reader?

Write down a list of the most vivid ideas and phrases in the book. You can then mix and match these to come up with a title. It may also help to use a thesaurus when doing this.

2. Research Keywords

As we've said, again and again, keywords are vitally important. You need to research what keywords people are looking for, and using **Publisher Rocket** (chapter 5) is the best tool to find out. Think about what people are most likely to type into the Amazon or Google search box, and enter those words into **PR**.

An excellent tool for doing keyword research is the Google Keyword Planner. This is a free tool that Google provides for doing keyword research. While there is a learning curve to using this tool, it's easy to figure out and provides accurate results. There are also dozens of other keyword tools which you may find helpful.

You can also use Google, Amazon, and YouTube search bars. Simply type in various words, phrases, and keywords. You want to pay attention to the words which are automatically filled in as well as the results which show up. Also, pay attention to the related searches section at the bottom of Google's results.

3. Draw up a List of Power Words

Defining exactly what power words are can be tricky. There's no clear definition, but these are some words that immediately grab your attention. They are forceful and convey a sense of power or deeper meaning. The following can be considered power words:

- Astonishing
- Breakthrough
- Discover
- Catastrophic
- Explosive
- Forced
- Gargantuan
- Humongous
- Incredible
- Killer

- Magic
- Nightmarish
- Obliterate
- Powerful
- Rare
- Secret
- Transform
- Unrelenting
- Voodoo
- Wow

A good place to find more of these words is in tabloid newspapers. Pay attention to the words used in the headlines of these newspapers. Think about the way they grab your attention, arouse curiosity, and evoke your emotions. Draw up a list of these power words and think about ways to use them in your title. Also, go through books in your niche and note any power words which are used.

4. Write Your Subtitle

Your title should be short, memorable, and to the point. The subtitle expands on this. Its purpose is to further explain what the book is about, list the benefits, create curiosity, build a connection with the reader, and include your keywords. In this way, you can almost think of the subtitle as a type of marketing slogan.

You should brainstorm at least 10-20 subtitles. Mix and match these subtitles until you come up with something that stands out. Also, look at the subtitles used by other books in your market.

5. Write Your Title

Finally, come up with a main title for the book. The most important thing when doing this is to have some type of hook. You need to come up with a phrase that will instantly stand out and grab your audience's attention. It needs to be eye-catching and make them stand up and say wow as they scan down the search results.

6. Test Your Title.

Once you've chosen several titles, test them. The way to do this is by setting up an advertising campaign on either Facebook or Google for a couple of days. It won't cost much at all. You can also use Twitter or any other advertising platform. Advertise your title and subtitle and see how many clicks you get. Whichever title gets the most attention should be your final choice.

7. Be Willing to Change Your Title

If your title isn't working, consider changing it. There's no reason you shouldn't, especially when your book isn't doing well. After all, when you're selling books online, it only takes a few clicks. Publishers have tested various titles for their books in doing their data research and discovered that by simply changing the name of a book, they could sometimes increase sales by 100%.

CHAPTER 7

Getting Started with Your Table of Contents and Structure

The key to excellent writing is creating a detailed outline and structure. It might sound cliché, but writing a book is exactly like building a house. Before starting, you need to draw up a blueprint. Know exactly what's going into the book and what you're going to write about.

Doing this has many benefits. It helps to prevent writer's block (*see chapter 10*), which sometimes occurs when you don't know where to go. It also gives you a series of points to work through. If you know the book will have ten chapters and each chapter is about X, Y & Z, then writing those chapters becomes much more manageable. All you have to do is fill in each chapter, and then you're done. Ultimately, a proper structure gives you something to aim for and makes your job a lot easier.

How to Write an Effective Outline for Your Book

There is no definite way to create an outline. But here are a few ideas to get you started.

1. Think in terms of "How-To" steps

As we've said, your book needs to deliver on a promise made to the reader. You've promised to help them solve a problem or achieve a specific goal. So, start your outline by thinking of the steps needed to solve this problem. What does the reader need to do to reach their goal? You can almost imagine you're writing one of those "how-to" articles you see online. Let's say you're writing a book about running your first marathon. In this case, your outline could include things like:

> **STEP 1:** What you need to know about running a marathon
> **STEP 2:** Determining your current fitness levels
> **STEP 3:** How long should you train before your first marathon
> **STEP 4:** Buying your first pair of running shoes
> And so on…

Keep going until you've completed all the steps involved in solving the problem.

2. Create a Broad Overview

Another way to structure your book is simply by sitting down and writing a broad overview. You can think of this as a business plan or mission statement for the book. Again, think about solving the problem or goal. Then write a broad 1000-2000-word explanation of how you would do this. Your overview can then be broken down into sections and expanded upon.

3. Use Mind Maps

There's no rule stating that your structure must comprise words. You can also create a visual structure using mind maps. Developing your outline this way is probably a good idea if you're not a writer. Something else you might want to try is dictating your ideas. Record ideas for the book onto your phone and then transcribe these later.

4. Simply Start Writing

Creating a detailed structure isn't absolutely necessary. While this helps, it's not something that you *have* to do. If you're struggling with the structure, then simply start writing. Start with the most important elements you can think of, then go from there. You'll probably notice that the pieces fall into place as you progress, and a structure slowly reveals itself.

5. Think About the Other Sections of Your Book

What else is going to go in the book besides the text? Are you planning to include pictures, drawings, checklists, case studies, or exercises? Are you going to create an index or write a foreword and afterword? Will you have an author bio or start each chapter with a quote? List these extras and then work on them. Doing this will make your life a lot easier. Maybe the first thing you'll write is your author bio. This can be an easy way to start the book.

6. Create Your Table of Contents

Writing the table of contents is one of the best ways to outline your book. The way to do this is with your subheadings. For example, buying a pair of running shoes is step four in running a marathon. Well, this step could probably be further broken down into more steps. Maybe you'll write about the different types of running shoes and the pros and cons of each type. Then you could write another section called '10 things to look for in a running shoe, or '5 ways to break in a running shoe without getting blisters. You basically want to list out your chapters and write as many subheadings as possible. From there, it's simply a case of filling in the information beneath those subheadings. Remember, you can always go back and reshuffle this table of contents and update it as you progress.

You also need to understand that your table of contents is critical. There are several reasons for this. The table of contents should be seen as a selling tool for the rest of the book. It creates curiosity about what's in the book, the benefits the reader will gain, and gives them a reason to read. This is especially important when you consider the Amazon look-inside feature. If you use this feature, one of the first things your reader will see is your table of contents. Writing an effective table of contents helps the customer decide to buy your book.

CHAPTER 8

The Writing - Dive In / Move Before You Are Ready

At this point, you've done your research, chosen a niche, come up with a title or a rough title for now, and created an outline. All that remains is to write the book. This is the hard part where you have to sit down and put pen to paper. You've spent all your time planning and thinking about the book and haven't written a word yet - and this can make you feel anxious or even afraid. What you have to understand is that these feelings are perfectly normal. It's something that every writer goes through. Just remember, once you get into the flow of it, it will be a therapeutic and immersive pursuit that you will start looking forward to.

You also need to understand that no one can do this for you. You need to just simply dive in and start filling out your chapters. Here are some tips to keep in mind that will help you through the writing process.

A) Move Before You Are Ready

Robert Greene is a famous author who wrote a book called 'The 50ᵗʰ Law' with rapper 50 Cent. In this book, he explains how 50 Cent's hustler and fearless mindset, which he learned from his upbringing in the ghetto, also got him out of the ghetto (where he was nearly murdered) and into fame and fortune. It also uses quotes and concepts from many great historical figures and leaders, such as Napoleon and Marcus Aurelius.

One of the best concepts in this book is to "move before you think you're ready." Doing this makes it a little more difficult for you, but in turn, you become more alert and focused. Because you are not quite prepared, you work harder and become more inventive. You must rise to the appropriate level, and you will.

This concept changed my life. It can be used in all aspects of life. If you think about it, nobody is ever ready for anything they do, especially if it's something new and outside their comfort zone. It's like signing up for a half marathon that takes place in two months. Even though you have no training done, you've now paid for the marathon and told people about it. This means you absolutely have to succeed and will train harder and be more focused.

It's the same with writing a book. You will never feel fully ready. So just dive in and start writing. Don't think too much about what you're doing and fall into analysis paralysis. Don't worry too much about punctuation or grammar. That can be edited and fixed later. Just get those first 1000 words done and start building momentum.

B) Stay Accountable to Yourself

It's critically important that you set goals and stay accountable to yourself. You need to set daily objectives and stick to them. Make a commitment that you'll write a certain number of words daily. This can be anything from 500 to 1000 or even 2000 words daily. Now, if you've never written anything, this might seem impossible. But what you should realize is that it gets easier. All you have to do is fight through the pain barrier. The more you write, the easier it gets, and after a little while - as long as you keep going - you'll start to enjoy it. The bottom line is that you need to stay consistent, and even if you just get 500 words done on some bad days, you are still moving forward in the right direction.

The reason accountability is so important because it allows you to set up a timeframe for yourself. By writing X amount of words per day, you can determine how long it will take to finish the book. Deadlines are crucial when writing a book. You should give yourself 30 to 60 days (90 at most) and then do your best to stick to this deadline. This has to be done if you're going to achieve your goal of finishing the book.

The exact opposite is also true. If you don't set daily

goals, it's easy to fall out of the habit of writing. Skip a day here or there, and those days turn into weeks and then months. Eventually, you lose interest and may even give up. I do not want this for you, and that's why it's so essential that you set and stick to these daily goals. Also, realize that writing is a habit. If you write every day, you'll quickly get into the habit of writing, and the whole process gets much easier.

C) You don't have to *Write*, but you do have to *Work*
While it's important to write every day, this isn't always possible. There are going to be days when you don't feel up to it. Days when you're exhausted from work, too busy, or simply can't think of anything to write. That's okay. It's something that happens to us all. But in those days, you should at least try to get something done and keep things moving forward.

This can mean many things. At the very least, you should read other books on your topic. You should also make an effort to read other fiction and also nonfiction books. As I mentioned in chapter 1, reading books helps you understand narrative arcs and may give you inspiration for new ideas. Study the layout and content of those books. Go onto Amazon and look through your category. See what's on the best-seller lists and read reviews for those books. Try to figure out what works and what doesn't for those books. Research your topic and try to come up with new ideas.

Something else you can do is revise your book. Go through what you've written so far and rewrite sections, paragraphs, and sentences. Use a thesaurus to find better or more exciting words. Run your work through grammar-checking programs like Grammarly. Something else you can do is work on your book's cover art or layout.

D) Stick to a Routine

Something that helps tremendously is sticking to a routine. It helps to write at the same time and place every day. This will also help you form the habit of writing. If you're writing outside of your home, then go to the same café every day. Sit in the same seat at the same time of day. Order the same coffee. Use the same laptop. All of this will further entrench the writing habit. I prefer writing in cafes that are spacious and have a calm vibe, usually on the outskirts of cities.

I look forward to this time, knowing I'm getting out of the house and doing something productive. Turn off your Wi-Fi on your phone for an hour or two so you don't have any unnecessary distractions.

These four ideas will help you with the psychological aspect of writing your book. I now want to mention more specific techniques that you can use while doing the actual writing.

1. Tell Stories Wherever Possible

Stories are extraordinarily powerful when used in nonfiction. The reason is simple. Stories get remembered and acted upon. They affect our emotions and help us build a connection with the reader. On the other hand, facts and figures are quickly forgotten. They are dry and boring and do not hold the readers' interest.

Try to present your information in story form wherever possible. The easiest way to do this is with personal stories. This is particularly powerful if you're helping the reader overcome a problem or challenge. For example, if your book is about running a marathon, then tell the story of your first marathon. If you're writing a meditation beginner's manual, then share your initial struggles with falling into the meditative state and how your mind was constantly racing elsewhere, but after time you began to love it, and it was effortless. Stories are also a great way to start your chapters. They help to draw the reader into the material and keep them reading until the end.

2. Use Cliff-Hangers

Cliff-hangers have been used for hundreds of years in fiction and should be inserted wherever you can. It's important that you use them where possible. Attention is a vital commodity in today's world of endless distractions. Just because someone has read your book doesn't mean they're going to finish it. To keep them going, you need to arouse their curiosity. They have to be curious enough to continue reading. Make them desperate to find out the answers to their questions. Never present your information in a dry and straightforward manner, and don't give the reader everything at once. Always do your best to tease them and make your audience curious enough to continue with the book.

3. Use Emotional Language

You never want your writing to be boring. It needs to be spellbinding, compelling, and utterly unforgettable. To achieve this goal, you need to use emotional language. Your text must contain vivid imagery which paints a clear mental picture. Try to put personality into your writing and use metaphors wherever possible. Refer to our section on power words in chapter 6. Remember, these words help to arouse the emotions of your reader. They get readers involved and engaged with your text, and it helps build a deeper connection with them. That being said, you don't want to overdo this. Use emotional language sparingly and avoid lapsing into purple prose. It's almost like seasoning a meal. Too much salt and the food is ruined.

4. Keep it Simple

In general, and particularly for nonfiction, you want to keep your writing style simple and straightforward. This is especially important if you're teaching or giving instructions. The reader should be able to understand what you're saying (try to cut down on jargon as much as possible). For the most part, focus on short sentences and simple words. Don't overcomplicate things too much. Write the way you speak and use plain language mixed in with emotional language. At the same time, mix up your sentences and contrast longer sentences with shorter ones.

Keep your paragraphs short and break the material down into sections that can be easily digested. You also want to avoid giving your reader too much information. Your explanations should be short, concise, and to the point.

Something else you should explore is the Flesch-Kincaid readability scale. This is basically a test designed to discern how difficult it is to read a piece of text. The test is measured out of a hundred, and various scores correspond to grade levels and, thus, reading ease. The higher your score, the easier it is to read the text. For example, a score of 100 equates to a 5th-grade level, which is pretty easy to read. A score of 60 equates to 12th grade, which is pretty difficult to read. You want to score somewhere between 70 and 100 on this scale. Scoring at this level means your text is easy enough for most people to understand.

There are many online tools that will grade the readability of your text.

5. Use Transition Phrases

Transition phrases are tiny phrases you can use at the start of your sentences. They help to increase readership and keep people moving through the text. They include things like:

- In addition to
- What's more
- Not only that
- More importantly
- At the same time

These phrases can be scattered throughout your text. They are most effective at the start of paragraphs and new sections.

6. Check your Facts

Everything you've written must be true and factual. Don't make things up. In order to have credibility as a writer, you need to tell the truth. It's also vital that you can back up what you say. Whenever you make a claim, be sure to back it up afterward. This is especially important if your book is about solving a particular problem. You need to prove you can solve that problem.

7. Chapters and Subheadings

This is the best way to start writing your book. With enough headings and subheadings, you will be able to write a chunk of words for each subheading, whether that's 200 or 500 words, or more. Usually, it will vary. Just remember that the first edit doesn't have to be perfect. Things can always get reshuffled and updated. Refer back to chapter 7 for more on this.

<u>Writing Hack</u>

Voice-to-text is a fantastic way to get your writing done quicker. Updated Microsoft Word should have this function, and if not, there are plenty of online tools to use this feature. The pros are that this is a lot faster than typing. The cons are that sometimes it will pick up the words you speak slightly wrong. And it's hard to think on the spot when you have nothing in front of you to read. It's best to jot down some bullet points written on paper and then use the voice-to-text tool from there.

INTERLUDE

At this point in the book, I have a small favor to ask. As there are many similar books in this category, I have learned that gathering reviews is hugely important. If you like what you have read so far, and it has brought some value and knowledge to your life, it would mean a lot if you could take 30 seconds of your time and head over to amazon and write a nice brief review. A sentence or two will do!

Just scan the QR code with your phone camera and it will take you straight to the review section.

*(if you are based in the UK or elsewhere, simply edit the **'.com'** to **'.co.uk'** or whatever relevant country code.)*

Thank you! By the way, this is something I recommend you do too with your future books.

I look forward to seeing your thoughts!

CHAPTER 9

The Art of Storytelling / Hero's Journey

In this chapter, we will be discussing storytelling and themes. Even though most people will be writing nonfiction, the subject of storytelling is still important. As we've already spoken about, it is vital to tell stories where possible in your writing. Stories are a memorable and powerful way to convey information. They also help to build a connection with your readership. They help to draw readers in and keep them reading until the end of your book.

For this reason, anything you write should follow the structure of a story. If your book is nonfiction, but you're writing about your account and experiences, this skill will help you tremendously. Storytelling principles, such as suspense, drama, and cliffhangers, are useful no matter what you're writing. This is especially important if you're writing fiction.

While writing stories may seem difficult to beginners, what you should realize is that almost all stories follow a particular pattern. In this way, stories can almost be seen as a type of music. As long as you follow specific "scales," it is relatively easy to write an engaging story.

For example, first, you draw the audience in by breaking comfort and rapport. Then comes the razzle-dazzle of excitement, suspense, drama, and developing relationships with certain characters. But the story can't be all crazy and fast-paced. That would be exhausting. There has to be a calm before another storm. This is so that you can get to know the characters on a deeper level and emphasize with them while the ideas and plot are taking shape and playing out. This also gives the reader breathing space and gives your work a feeling of plausibility.

Finally, you want to ramp things up toward the end of the book before wrapping it all up and a unique lesson after the grand finale. This leaves the reader feeling satisfied and complete. As if they have been on a journey themselves.

Stephen King is quoted as saying, *"good books don't give you all their secrets at once."* Open loops, suspense, plot twists, and cliffhangers all leave the reader wanting more. This is what all good books and stories should have. Another great quote from Anton Chekhov is, *'don't tell me the moon is shining, show me the Clint of light on Broken Glass'*.

The Hero's Journey Storytelling Structure:
Probably the most well-known story structure is the so-called **Hero's Journey**. This name was coined by academic Joseph Campbell in 1949. Stories that follow this structure have three distinct stages.

1. The Departure Stage
The hero leaves behind their ordinary life and enters a special world, where they embark on a grand adventure.

2. The Initiation Stage
The hero then journeys into unknown territory and is transformed through various trials and challenges. Along the way, they also learn many lessons from various mentors and guides.

3. The Return Stage
The hero returns home in triumph and passes on his wisdom.

Hundreds of writers have successfully used this structure in books, novels, plays, and movies. One of the best examples is the story of Luke Skywalker in Star Wars. Think about his journey from naïve farm boy to Jedi Master. His quest through the galaxy and the challenges and obstacles he overcame. His time spent learning from wise master Yoda and his eventual triumph over the forces of evil.

Lord of the Rings

Another great example is Frodo Baggins from the Lord of the Rings. He starts off in the ordinary world of the shire and is suddenly tasked with great responsibility. There is fear connected to this calling and the terror of entering unknown places. He doesn't want to do it. Moving beyond his comfort zone is difficult.

But then, he meets a mentor in the form of Gandalf, the tall gray-bearded wizard. Now he has to crossover from the ordinary world into a special world where there is adventure and danger. In your own book, this can represent a challenging experience you encountered and had to overcome. Maybe this was the experience of losing weight, transforming your body, or getting out of debt. It could be the experience of changing jobs or moving somewhere new.

Then comes the drama, the tests, the battles, and the ups and downs. You fight various enemies but also have allies who help you in times of difficulty. All of these events are building up to some type of finally. An enormous challenge or ordeal. And in the end, you come through it.

Frodo reaches Mount Doom despite all the obstacles he faces along the way. He destroys the ring, and Sauron's power is now gone. Frodo triumphs, and the world is saved. At the end of *Hero's Journey*, like at the end of the Lord of the Rings, there is always a kind of symbolic road back home, back to the Shire. This gives the reader time to think about the lessons Frodo and the other characters have learned and the knowledge they may want to pass on in the future.

Your Personal Story

You could have a story about living a completely normal life until something turns your world upside down. It may be a health scare, an accident, an epiphany, or anything. Suddenly, you're thrown into the unknown with all the fears and anxiety that come with that. There is now a sense of urgency and a profound reason to change your current circumstances. Perhaps your doctor warns you that you might only have 5 - 10 years left to live if you continue your current unhealthy lifestyle.

Enormous challenges and obstacles are thrown your way, but with the help of others, with researching and learning new habits and skills, you take on these challenges and rise above them. Although hugely difficult in the beginning, you manage to get yourself fit and healthy. Better still, you became addicted to that feeling of having more energy, and you begin to run marathons and set up 10 km fundraising events. You meet new people and new friends. You lead a whole new life now with a fresh outlook on everything. When all is said and done, you look back to see how far you've come and wonder if you can pass on this knowledge and inspiration to someone else who may need the same help and advice you wish you had sooner.

I'm sure you can see the complete *Hero's Journey* cycle within that example. It's not an uncommon story, and so many people have had an event in their life that spurred them into action and changed their lives for the better. It also doesn't have to take a significant event to create massive change in your life. Getting healthy is just one example of thousands. But it's a clear example of how *Hero's Journey* is a part of almost every good story, whether fiction or nonfiction. So it's important to keep it in mind when writing your book.

Creative Writing Exercise
Right now, you may still be wondering, *"But I don't have a life-changing story to tell, so how do I incorporate storytelling and this structure into a story about having my breakfast or my weekend trip to Budapest?"* As a creative exercise, I want you to try it out. This isn't nearly as difficult as it may seem. Start by writing down the boring version of your story first. Once that's done, spice things up and flesh it out. Think about how you can change things to conform to the hero's journey structure. Add drama and suspense to the language, even if it seems exaggerated or ironic. Don't pressurize yourself, and remember to have fun. Here is an example of turning a boring, mundane story about having breakfast into something dramatic, fun, and engaging.

"As I trudged downstairs and opened the fridge door, to my shock and horror, the lid on the milk carton was missing! Now the milk is gone off and useless! I also realize that someone has stolen all the bananas. How will I survive my day without my trusted porridge, milk, and banana mix? How will I function properly? I have an important presentation for my boss at 11 am. Then I suddenly remembered how, 500 years ago, just a blip in time, there was no porridge, nor were there fridges to keep milk

fresh and readily available in fancy plastic containers. People went for hours in the morning foraging and searching for food. They didn't complain. In fact, it strengthened them physically and mentally. Breathe. Just grab a protein bar on the way to work. Okay, I think I will survive this morning's presentation. Actually, I'm going to knock it out of the park! First-world problems. Today is going to be a good day. I can feel it. It's all about the attitude you bring".

As you can see, I just transformed a story about me missing breakfast one morning into something far more dramatic and uplifting. Was it a bit ridiculous? Most definitely. But writing this part of this book was so much fun for me. I wrote that piece in almost one take. It put me in a creative state, and I wasn't thinking about the outcome. This is why I love writing so much and keep re-emphasizing how anyone can do this and how it is immersive and is the ideal pursuit.

Now, if that's what can be achieved with a story about eating breakfast with one take, imagine what can be done with the actual content of your own personal story or book idea. The potential is endless.

Another helpful exercise is practicing your storytelling in real life. The easiest way to do this is by turning boring conversations into exciting ones. Whether at a party or an event or simply talking to your friends. Instead of asking someone, *"what's your job"* ask, *"what are your passions?"* Do the same if someone asks you this question. Talk about your passions rather than speaking about your job title.

Think about your job and the city you're from. Think of ways to make them sound exciting.

You can practice on a Dictaphone or in front of a mirror. These ways will help you sound like a more exciting and interesting person and can help you in social situations or even with things like interviews. All skilled storytellers and public speakers will tell you it's all in the mannerisms—the gestures—The eye contact, and voice tonality, whether that means going from a high to a low pitch or speeding up and slowing down.

If you can practice doing all of this, it will significantly improve your writing and storytelling ability. So as an exercise, just take a dull story, like talking about what you had for lunch, and turn it into a story full of turns, twists, anticipation, and drama.

Story Cubes
Something else you might want to experiment with is Rory's Story Cubes. These are a series of dice which have pictures on them. You roll the dice and make up a story by using the pictures on each dice. This is a fun and simple way to improve your storytelling abilities. I've used these cubes myself, and with daily practice, they really do improve your ability to tell stories.

CHAPTER 10

Writer's Block - Practical Ways to Overcome it

One of the biggest obstacles to finishing your Ebook is writer's block. Sometimes you will hit a mental roadblock and struggle to write even a single word. This could happen 2 or 3 days in a row or even when the book is 90% complete. This happens to every writer at one time or another and isn't something you should worry about too much.

So how do you overcome this and continue writing your book? First, you must realize that writer's block is inside your head. Now, that may sound like a flippant thing to say. If you're struggling to write, you probably want something more concrete. What it essentially comes down to is overcoming your mental blockages. The truth about writer's block is that it's a form of performance anxiety. You can't write because you're worried about what you're writing, not the physical act of writing itself.

Think of it like this. Imagine yourself as a musician. You're performing in front of a crowd of people. There's a great deal of pressure to perform, and because of this, you're getting stuck in your head and struggling to play. Now imagine you're sitting alone in a room, playing freestyle solos with the instrument with no concern about how you're playing or how it sounds. You're relaxed and free of all stress. This is the mindset you should have when writing. Writer's block is created because you're trying too hard. You're constantly worried about your performance and trying to come up with something brilliant.

It doesn't matter what you write as long as you're writing something. In fact, when you have writer's block, what you write doesn't matter at all. If you're struggling to come up with something, then start writing random nonsense off the top of your head. Remember, it absolutely does not matter what you write. All that's important is that you're writing (and having fun while doing it).

Something else to remember is that whatever you write will be edited later anyway. You're going to write, rewrite, and edit your work over and over again, so it really doesn't matter what you put down initially. All that matters is that you write *something*. The reason for writer's block is that people try to get it right the first time. They're too concerned with coming up with something brilliant and perfect the first time around. And they get stuck in their head and develop writer's block.

Another reason people develop writer's block is that they lack experience. The fact is that if you want to become an experienced writer, if you want to get good at this, then you have to write and write a lot. You may have to write tens of thousands of words before you truly develop a knack for this. Then eventually, it becomes second nature and effortless. Until then, you may get frustrated from time to time, but that's ok. It's all part of the learning process.

Compare this to professional writers who may have to come up with thousands of words per day. Sometimes they do this day in and out for years. These people also experience writer's block. But when they do, they are calm and know it will soon pass. They have the skills and tools to deal with it and overcome it.

Writing is an abstract pursuit. It's not like building a wall where you have to follow a particular set of steps. Writing is a creative, artistic endeavor, meaning there is no step by step one size fits all solution to this problem. Ultimately, it's up to you to break through the barriers and overcome any issues you may face.

Another reason people develop writer's block is often that they're stressed out, tired, anxious, or exhausted. Sometimes you just need to take a break. Whatever problem you're facing, here are a few things you can do;

Here Are Some Ways Famous Authors Overcome Writer's Block:

1. Take a Hike

When it comes to being more creative, there's nothing better than getting out into the fresh air and sunshine. Doing this will get your creative juices pumping. When you return to your desk at the end of the day or the next day, you'll feel relaxed, revitalized, and ready to write.

Hiking also helps to bring you into the present moment. It will more or less consume your whole day. Your attention and focus will be on the present moment and what's directly in front of you. Because hiking can be somewhat dangerous depending on the weather and terrain, you need to be alert at all times. For this reason, the last thing you'll be thinking about is your book and what you need to write about.

This works as a marvelous reset button for your creative flow of energy. If you don't want to hike, many other physical activities can bring you into the present moment. For example, you can go for a swim, walk along the beach, go for a run, or even lift weights in the gym. These activities will take your mind off writing and help to renew your creative flow.

2. Play

Playing games is another terrific way to distract your mind from writing difficulties. It doesn't matter what games you play. They can be video games, board games, puzzles, cards, or anything else. Play also doesn't necessarily mean you have to play games. You simply want to find some type of activity that will distract you from work. For example, painting, cooking, baking, gardening, and dozens of other activities can help get your mind out of your funk. Make sure it's something light and fun.

You simply want to let your mind wander and go on autopilot while you're playing or doing your chosen hobby. Often people can become anxious and feel like they're wasting time doing something like this. Nothing could be further from the truth. Don't forget about your subconscious mind. Much of what you write comes from your subconscious. By taking time out to play, you refresh your subconscious. This helps your conscious mind to focus on the business of writing. You may also find that new ideas come to you seemingly out of nowhere after taking part in a creative hobby outside of writing.

3. Listen to Music

Music can be a powerful catalyst for creativity. The reason is purely scientific. Music comprises sound waves, which can have a powerful effect on your psychology. Think back to the last time you listened to a moving piece of music. Remember the way the hairs on your arms stood up and the way the music affected your emotions and shifted your mindset.

Music is a great way to get yourself out of mental ruts and is something that you should utilize as often as possible. Also, don't be afraid to dance to your favorite tunes. Doing this gets your juices flowing and may help you break through creative barriers. You'll also probably want to put together a playlist of music you can listen to while working on your book. Radio and Hit music don't really go well with writing. The music is too intense and distracting. You are better off going for something like 'progressive house or 'minimal techno. Shingo Nakamura is my go-to DJ for writing. Hours-long of calm but catchy house music that blends perfectly. Some people go for particular sounds and binaural beats. YouTube is your friend, so browse around and see what suits you best.

4. Socialize with Friends and Family

One downside to writing is that you usually spend enormous amounts of time alone. After a while, this can have adverse effects on your mental health. You don't want to become a complete hermit. Therefore, it's crucial that you spend time with people who make you feel good. Whether these are family members or friends, try to get out of the house and spend time with people whom you like, who give you energy.

5. Yoga or Meditation

Yoga and meditation are tools that every writer should utilize. Both practices are highly beneficial for improving your mental state. They can quickly put you in a different frame of mind and redirect your focus and energies somewhere more positive. Not only that, but yoga is great for loosening the body up and stretching all the joints and muscles that can become tight from sitting in one position for too long. This will revitalize your body, filling you with more energy.

6. Change the Environment You're Working in

I did mention earlier to stick to a routine and go to the same coffee shop or same location every time you write. But when in a funk, a change is as good as a holiday. It can also help your creativity. You can stimulate new ideas and restore your creative flow by changing your environment. So consider changing up your writing location for a short time. Move from your study or bedroom into the lounge or kitchen. Change up the coffee shop you've been writing in or go to a library on the other side of town. (you may also want to explore writing in a co-working space). Changing your environment and going somewhere new can create a more stimulating work environment. You can feed off the energy of that environment, especially if you're in a busy part of town or near a university. I love having my headphones on and watching all the different characters coming in and out, ordering coffee while I sit snug in the corner working on my project. It beats sitting at home in your office every day and for me, it's far more productive. But everyone is different. With a good attitude, you can write anywhere.

7. Eliminate all Distractions

To write well, you need to enter a type of Zen state. Achieving this state means all distractions must be removed. Turn off your phone's Wi-Fi or put it on silent. Stop listening to the radio or watching TV. Lock your door. Close the curtains. All of this is worth trying and will definitely help. Remember, the goal here is to overcome writer's block, and experimentation is key.

8. Noise-Canceling Headphones

Noise-canceling headphones can really benefit your writing, especially if you're someone who is easily distracted and just enjoys solitude. I am a bit of a tech freak and have experimented with almost every brand of headphones and AirPods there is. But by far, one of my best purchases has been Bose noise-canceling headphones from Amazon. I literally use these everywhere I go. They were totally worth the money. They block out the sound when I want silence and solitude (like when I'm writing), and the sound quality when I play music is exceptional. It can be a surreal experience walking around a busy city or café and just hearing absolute silence.

Here are the specific ones I use if you are interested:

US

UK:

8. Read

I once read the quote, *"Reading is like breathing in, and writing is like breathing out."* These words contain an enormous amount of wisdom. If you want to be a writer, you need to read as much as possible. Read everything that you can, from classic literature to low-brow pulp. Read fiction and nonfiction, magazines, newspapers, and internet articles. Whatever chance you get. Doing this should help to stimulate your creativity. Again, it will also teach you what good and bad writing looks like and give you a standard of writing for which you should aim.

9. Brainstorm Ideas

Just because you've sat down to write doesn't mean you have to write. Developing new ideas is an equally valuable use of your time. If you're stuck, spend some time thinking about what you actually want to write. Think about some new directions you could take with your book. Maybe you could come up with an alternative beginning or ending. Perhaps you could add a new bonus chapter. You can also revise what you've already written in your writing time.

10. Motivate Yourself

Your writer's block could also be due to a simple lack of motivation. If this is the case, read something inspiring. Motivational quotes are always an excellent choice. Another good choice is motivational videos on YouTube. There are thousands to choose from, and they may help get you back into the flow of things.

CHAPTER 11

Finishing Details - Peer Checks, Edits, Layout, Illustrations, and Cover

By now, your book should be 90% complete. You've done the hard work and reached the home stretch. All that remains is checking over the work and turning your manuscript into a finished book. I highly recommend hiring professionals such as freelancers from **Fiverr** or **Upwork** to help you with this process. The process of finalizing your book contains several steps:

1. Let the Book Sit for a While
Once your book is written, take a short break. Leave it

alone for a week and try to forget about it. When you come back, read through the manuscript once again. Edit anything that immediately jumps out at you. This is important. When looking at your writing with fresh eyes, you'll more than likely find many things to change or update.

2. Peer Check

Next, get a second opinion on the book. You want to give the book to as many people as possible and have them read through it. You need to know what people think of your work and get feedback on what you've done. It helps to share your book with people who are involved in the topic you've written about. If you wrote a book about meditation, try to find someone who meditates. If your book is about running a marathon, then get feedback from other marathon runners.

One thing you need to remember during this process is that you cannot get your ego involved. Take all criticism with an open mind. Also, make sure that your peers are not just being polite and praising you. Sit down with them and talk about the book. Force them to give you some constructive criticism and feedback. They may suggest rearranging parts or changing up the style of certain sections. Remember, the first draft will always be far from perfect. You're going to have to make some changes regardless, so you cannot let your pride get in the way. That being said, your first draft, most certainly, won't be as bad as you think if you walk away from it for a while and come back to it.

You may also want to get feedback from outside your peer group. Let's be honest: friends and family are not the best choices for critics. While they may point at grammatical errors and things of that nature, they're unlikely to give you any hard criticism. If your book sucks, friends and family are the last people who will tell you. What you need is outside criticism. One of the easiest ways to do this is by going online. There are dozens of online resources for checking and criticizing your work. Sites like Fiverr.com and Upwork.com are great places to find beta readers. You also can reach out to people from Facebook groups related to your book topic.

3. Line and Copy Edit

Before publishing the book, you need to have it professionally edited. This will help to polish the text and get it ready for publication. The abovementioned sites can also be used to find editors. Ideally, you want to hire two people. One freelancer will do the line edit. This person looks at punctuation, spelling, and grammar. The other freelancer should be someone who knows about your niche topic. This person will do the copy edit. What that means is that they look at the paragraphs, themes, and ideas in the book. This person will suggest changes or even new material.

So after getting feedback and editing the book yourself, you'll want to let it sit for a bit longer. Then go back to it with fresh eyes and add any changes your copy editor suggested. After that, give it back to your line editor so that they can double-check your spelling and grammar.

You may also want to simply edit the book yourself. You'll probably want to do this if you're on a tight budget (depending on the length of your book, editors can be expensive). If you go this route, start by printing the book out, as this will make things easier. Go through the manuscript line by line with a ruler and correct any mistakes you find. You might want to do this while sitting in front of your computer and making changes to the document itself. This will save you time. Otherwise, make those corrections on the printout. It's definitely advised to use an editor software such as **Grammarly**. While the free version will pick up a lot of mistakes, the premium version, which costs roughly $30 a month, will pick up on everything and suggest clearer sentences that flow better. However, the free version is still a great place to start. And if you do go for the premium version, $30 is far cheaper than hiring an editor, which can cost anywhere from $200 upwards, depending on how long your book is.

When self-editing, there are several things you should consider:

a. **Change Words and Sentences** - try to use better and more vivid words to improve your sentences. Don't repeat the same words too often. Cut down sentences that are too long or overly wordy.

b. **Change Sections** - improve the flow and structure of your sections. Change things around and make everything as clear as possible. The reader's journey through the book should be straightforward and logical. At no point should the reader be confused. Look out for places where you may have repeated yourself.

c. **Make it Personal** - cut out sections that are too technical and do not connect with the reader. Find ways to involve the reader and use stories where you can.

d. **Check Facts and Quotes** - double and triple-check your facts. Add references where you can. Add in extra material if necessary.

e. **Use Grammar Checkers** - you should also run your text through grammar-checking software. There are several free solutions online, and as I've said earlier, Grammarly is the best of the bunch.

f. **Read the Book Out Loud** - this is a technique recommended by many writers. Reading your work out aloud helps you improve the flow of your sentences. It also allows you to cut down sentences that may be unnecessarily long. This technique will also help you pick up mistakes you may have missed. Reading the book aloud is also a good idea if you're planning to record an audiobook. It's a good run-through for the audiobook and helps you determine if your material is suitable for recording.

After working through these points, put the book away for another week or so. Then take it out and go through this editing process again. Keep doing this until you feel your book cannot be improved more.

4. Cover Art and illustrations

They say that a book should never be judged by its cover, but unfortunately, this rarely happens. The fact is that the cover is an integral part of what makes a book sell. If the cover is not high-quality, you will have a hard time finding buyers.

This is especially true for fiction, and more specifically, genre fiction. Anyone who reads fantasy, sci-fi, or romance books will already know this. These books often have highly detailed cover art, and it is this fantastic imagery that often helps to sell the book. Even if you've written a nonfiction book, it helps to have excellent cover art. You want something eye-catching and attractive. You also need good-quality illustrations. Remember, the better your illustrations, the higher the perceived quality of the book will be. Your book may only have a few illustrations, so ensure they are good.

To do this, you'll again want to hire a freelancer from Fiverr.com. It's a good idea to test styles from different freelancers on the website. Check through samples of their work and see if they're a good fit. Does their art impress you, and is it a good fit for your style of book? Also, look at the competition. Your cover should be better, brighter, and stand out amongst the crowd.

5. Layout

Finally, when you're 100% ready, send the manuscript off to a layout person. If you intend to make your book into a paperback, you can order a proof copy and have one last look through the book. Go through it line by line and look for grammatical or spelling errors. Now you are ready to publish. It's an amazing feeling. Once you go through this process and experience it, you'll be able to do it again and again.

6. Publishing on KDP

The first place you should publish your book is on KDP, as Amazon is the biggest book market in the world currently. It is very simple and straightforward. First, it's best to upload the Ebook version. To make sure your Ebook looks okay, download the free Kindle Previewer app and upload your word document or PDF. Here you can preview how your book will look on a tablet, a smartphone, and a Kindle E-reader. Then simply begin the process of uploading the document to KDP. There are many simple tutorials on KDP and YouTube to assist you in doing this. The paperback version will be a different document, as your layout will be different depending on the size you want for your book. But both processes are similar. It is not too complicated. You then decide what price you want to sell your book for all the different marketplaces. Within a couple of days, your book should be approved for sale.

It really is a great feeling! Especially the first time you do it. You will now have a product of value for sale across the world, and you can begin to be financially rewarded for your efforts.

CHAPTER 12

Ghostwriting

Having read this far through the book, many people will be filled with a sense of excitement. You're probably daydreaming about the book you're going to write and are ready to start. On the other hand, many of you may feel uncertain, confused, and overwhelmed by the amount of work that needs to be done. This chapter is for you if you're one of these people. Unfortunately, some people don't have the time or are not cut out to be writers. This doesn't mean you can't make a living publishing Ebooks. All it means is that you'll have to hire a ghostwriter.

What You Need to Know About Ghostwriting

A ghostwriter is essentially someone who writes for you. This can include anything, from writing novels to technical manuals or even blog posts. The key distinction is that your name goes on the final product. The ghostwriter is paid a flat fee, and any money you receive from book sales is entirely yours. The best example of ghostwriting is celebrity biographies. These celebrity ghostwriters can charge thousands of dollars for their work. Luckily for you, there is a much cheaper option.

You also need to understand that just because you hire a ghostwriter doesn't mean you don't have to put in any work. You cannot simply hire a writer, give them a topic, and hope for the best. It's necessary to provide an outline that contains as much detail as possible. This way, your writer will be able to produce a book you're happy with.

This is an important point. The power of ghostwriting is that it gives you time to focus on other things besides the grunt work of writing. One of these things is research. Hiring a writer means you are free to research the topic to a greater degree. You can learn what the market really wants, what topics could be written about, and ultimately what should go in the book. You're free to read similar and best-selling books about the subject. You can track down articles and blog posts that will help your writer.

What's most important is that you create a killer table of contents and a detailed outline for your ghostwriter. Tell them what kind of tone and vibe you are looking for. Show them the pros and cons of other similar bestselling books by looking at 3-star reviews of those books. Do all the data research as mentioned in Chapters 4 and 5. This means that your ghostwriter can now focus solely on the quality of writing rather than doing all the research on top of writing. Ghostwriting also means you have time to do other things, like working on the editing, cover, and illustrations. It also gives you time to focus on how you're going to market your book.

How to Find a Ghostwriter

Quality ghostwriters can be found online. If you look hard enough, you will find a writer with excellent reviews for around $400-800. You should be able to get a high standard 20,000-40,000-word book written for this amount of money. This is a fair price to pay for a full book to be written for you. These people are often up-and-coming writers. If you can afford to pay more, that's good too, that's your choice. Just be aware that paying extra does not automatically relate to a better quality of work in this field.

Hotghostwriter

Ghostwriting companies offer a great way to scale your publishing business quickly. A good company can bring you great writers and make the entire process streamlined. One of the most popular companies is Hotghostwriter.com

They call themselves "The self-publisher's official ghostwriting service" because their entire business is catered to publishers. Here are some of the main benefits of working with HGW, as pointed out by the company:

Quality

They're known for housing some of the best talents across many genres. Being one of the most premium services allows them to attract premium writers and deliver great books, essential for building a more long-term brand.

They have also rated 4.8 / 5 stars on <u>trustpilot</u> which reinforces their reputation.

One-Stop-Shop

Besides writing, Hotghostwriter offers pretty much all else you'll need to release a book to market. Some services include editing, cover design, book description writing, book formatting, audiobook narration, and more. All in one place.

Open Communication

Unlike most writing companies where the company essentially plays "middle-man" in communication, slowing things down, Hotghostwriter advocates for "open communication" with their team. That means you can directly interact with your writers, editors, designers, and more on their platform. This is great for brainstorming ideas and building relationships with your creatives, whilst making things ways more efficient in the process.

Live Project Access

Not only is communication open, but you can also access your book file live Via the cloud. You can in theory and watch your book being written in real-time. Great if you want to follow along, add ideas and comments, or simply ensure everything is on track.

Unlimited Revisions

A final real selling point is the fact that they offer unlimited revisions across most of their services, and this gives you the peace of mind they'll take care of anything you need and that you'll get a product you're happy with in the end.

I contacted HGW personally and was granted an exclusive special discount for readers of this book.

Use code **NW101** at checkout for 5% off your first order.

Freelancers

Another option is finding a ghostwriter on freelancer sites such as **Upwork** or **Fiverr**. Whichever platform you choose, it's critical that you go with someone who has excellent reviews. It's also important that you see samples of their work and interview the person thoroughly. Ask questions about their background and experience, and find out if they fully understand your topic. Also, don't rush into this. After you've found a selection of candidates, sleep on it a while before making your final decision.

These sites also have drawbacks, the biggest being that you have to do a bit more legwork compared to HGW.

You need to post your job offer, wait for proposals, and then interview people. This takes time. Also, unlike specialty ghostwriting sites, there's no set price. Your freelancer may try to haggle or negotiate with you for a higher price. You may also get into disputes or arguments over the work. But if you look hard enough, you can find high-quality writers here too.

What you should understand is that a lot of this comes down to experience. It may take a while to get the hang of things and find a writer you click with. Generally, these freelancers are good professional people, so you shouldn't encounter difficulties too often. It will also be worth taking your time to get the right fit for you, as the quality of your book is all that counts.

Alternatives to Ghostwriting

If you can't afford a ghostwriter or don't want to hire one, there are other alternatives to writing. The simplest way is to basically record your thoughts on the topic. This technique is recommended for people who are experts on a certain topic or otherwise highly passionate. Anyone with in-depth knowledge of a topic should be able to talk about that topic for hours.

Simply sit down with some type of recording device and start talking about the subject. Pretend you're giving a lecture or explaining the topic to a friend. You'll probably find that it takes a while to get started, but you soon warm up and have plenty to say. Keep going and explain everything there is to know about your topic or problem. You'll probably have to talk for several hours until you've enough material for a book. Have a list of bullet points for chapters or subheadings. Then speak on those points. Once this is done, you can get the recording transcribed or even transcribe it yourself. From there, you will have a rough draft of your book! Yes, it will take a hard edit, with a lot of rearranging and updating. But the bulk of the grunt work is done. The content has been created.

CHAPTER 13

Self-Publishing across Multiple Platforms / Audiobooks

There are dozens of advantages to publishing Ebooks. The biggest is that there are so many ways to profitably sell your books. When compared to traditional publishing, there's no competition. In fact, with traditional publishing being the way it is, you're lucky to make any money at all.

Why it's a Good Idea to Avoid Traditional Publishers
The average author advance is between $6000-$10,000. What makes this worse is that these are often an advance on royalties. This means you'll have to earn this money

back before you get any of it. Also, because traditional publishers are struggling, book advances are shrinking every year. Many authors receive far less than the abovementioned price - many receive nothing. Add to this the fact that royalty rates are abysmal. In most cases, you'll receive 7-25% or less.

Another disadvantage of traditional publishing is that you have to make your way through a gauntlet of editors, managers, and other gatekeepers. Unless you have an agent, it's unlikely that your manuscript will ever be seen (let alone approved). That's not to mention the editing process your book will have to go through. It could be years before you're published. Also, consider the fact that you may lose creative control. That you could easily find yourself in a situation where the publishing companies dictate what you write. I don't know about you, but I would never want to be in this situation. To make things worse, you'll have to sign a contract and this can have serious consequences. You never know what could be in the fine print, waiting to trip you up.

The only real advantage to traditional publishing is print distribution. A traditional publisher can get your book into bookstores. You will also receive a marketing budget, which helps to sell your book, as well as cover designers, layout specialists, and editors. However, these advantages are also falling by the wayside. Authors are forced to do their own marketing, and publishers are looking for authors who already have a platform. They want to sign people who have social media followers, subscribers on YouTube, or some type of online presence.

These publishing companies are basically looking for people who are already semi-famous and have a built-in audience for their books. For most ordinary authors, this is extremely difficult to achieve. And why should you go through the trouble of doing this when self-publishing is so much easier? Besides, if you develop an online presence, you're far better off using it to promote your self-published books. Why should you go through all the time and effort and then allow the publishing company to use it for their own benefit? It really doesn't make sense.

The only advantage to traditional publishing is ego validation. Many people feel that to be an actual author; they have to publish the traditional way. That self-publishers are amateurs; they're not "real" authors. They're not good enough to get published the traditional way.

Of course, that's utter nonsense. The world has changed, and self-publishing is the way of the future. Think about it - the publishing houses need you more than you need them, and unfortunately, traditional publishing no longer offers any advantage to skilled writers. It all boils down to this: do you want your ego stroked, or do you want to make a living as a writer? Are you pursuing fame and fortune and literary awards, or do you want to practice the craft of writing?

The Benefits of Self-Publishing

The benefits of self-publishing are countless. The biggest is that you have complete control over your work. From the title to your choice of cover, price, release date, and how the work is edited. There is no one to interfere with your work besides yourself. This level of freedom can be enormously empowering, and it's the reason many people choose the self-publishing route. Another huge advantage is that self-publishing is faster. There's absolutely no reason you shouldn't have your first book released within 30, 60, or 90 days. With traditional publishers, it could be years before your book goes live.

By far, the most important reason you should self-publish is potential income. With self-publishing, you'll receive about 70% of your book's cover price. Traditional publishers usually pay between 7-25%. You'll need to sell far fewer books to make the same amount of money. You'll also receive this money immediately, whereas, with publishers, you may have to wait until the end of the year or quarter. Worst of all, traditional publishers may not even be interested in your book. This will definitely be the case if you're writing about a niche subject with a tiny audience. Why not sell directly to your market?

Of course, self-publishing is not without its disadvantages. Unless you're using a ghostwriter, it can be a bit more work. Many writers have this romantic idea of living the writer's life. They see themselves in some exotic location, doing very little other than writing or navel-gazing. Unfortunately, if you want to be a successful self-published author, you're going to have to put in the work. You should see yourself as an entrepreneur or business person as much as a writer. Your goal is to make a living in the publishing business rather than to be an artist.

There can also be a tremendous learning curve, and you may have to master several disciplines. On top of this, you might have to invest your own money. You'll have to employ editors, cover designers, and other freelancers. Many people simply don't have the time and resources for this. If that's the case, then you may be better off with a traditional publisher.

Even if you do feel this way, self-publishing is the best way to get your foot in the door. If you're a successful self-published author, agents and publishers will beat a path to your door. You'll be courted by these people and get a far better deal than you would have otherwise.

Something else you'll miss out on is distribution in bookstores. The bookstores are dominated by traditional publishers. While it is possible to get your book into stores, it's a lot harder for self-published authors. Instead, your books will primarily be distributed through print-on-demand services. Finally, you'll miss out on literary acclaim. Most literary prizes don't accept self-published works, and literary critics turn their noses up at indie authors (although this isn't something you have to worry about if your book is nonfiction).

Different Book Formats for Maximum Income:

No matter how you decide to publish, it's imperative that you maximize your income. As we've said, you need to look at your book as a piece of intellectual property, which you can use to make money in various ways. What you essentially want to do is sell your content in as many different ways as possible. The easiest way to do this is by selling your book in different formats. These include:

1. Ebooks

This is the most common way to sell books on the internet. Ebooks provide you with many advantages—the biggest being that they can be instantly downloaded. Ebooks are essentially free to manufacture. There are literally infinite copies of your Ebook. This means you do not have to pay to have them produced.

2. Paperbacks

Even though most online sales will be Ebooks at the beginning, the most profitable sales will be for your paperbacks. This, of course, is for people who want a "real" version of the book. For nonfiction, in particular, most people prefer to buy the paperback version. Paperbacks can also be helpful for marketing purposes, especially if you're doing live events. Most authors use print-on-demand services these days. Examples of these services include Amazon KDP and IngramSpark. You can order author copies of your book for the price of the print production only. Usually, this will only be $3-4 each. The most significant advantage of these services is that only a single copy of the book is printed and then mailed to the customer. This means you don't get stuck with hundreds of books that you've printed yourself at home. These services also take care of postage, customer service, and everything else. It is all completely automated once set up.

3. Hardbacks

If you want to be fancier, it's also possible to do a 'print-on-demand hardback. These can be used if you're selling a special edition or early print run. You might want to offer a hardback version of your book because you can sell it at a far greater price point.

4. Workbooks
Workbooks are a great option for nonfiction authors. If your book has a Q&A section or other types of exercises, then these can easily be adapted into a workbook format.

Increase Sales by Publishing on Multiple Platforms:
The easiest way to make more money with your book is to simply publish it across multiple platforms. As we've said before, Amazon is the biggest platform and makes up 60% of the market. However, there are many other platforms that make up the remaining 40%.

These include sites like:

- IngramSpark
- iBooks
- PublishDrive
- Barnes & Noble Press
- Author's Republic
- Draft2Digital
- Lulu
- BookBaby
- ClickBank
- Gumroad
- Smashwords
- Kobo

Each platform has its pros and cons and is worth checking out. Also, don't forget you're perfectly capable of selling the book on your own website, too. We'll discuss this a bit more in the next chapter. Once you publish your book on Amazon and these other platforms, a lot of your hard work is complete. You're going to make sales no matter how small. Of course, all the platforms take a cut of your sales, but this is negligible, considering the income is passive. You don't have to do any maintenance or extra work unless you want to update your book cover or manuscript. The bottom line is that you've created a piece of intellectual content and can begin financially benefiting from it forever.

If your aim is to maximize your income, then research is the best way to do it. As we spoke about in previous chapters, find out which niches are hot and in the most demand. Learn about keywords and Amazon SEO. Collect data and look for market opportunities. From there, you can write the book yourself or create an outline for your ghostwriter. Another way to increase your earnings is by improving your cover, illustrations, and title. An impressive title and subtitle can dramatically boost your sales. Also, remember that most people prefer having paperbacks or even hardback books. Although the tide is changing, and many people like the convenience of Ebooks, there is still an enormous market for actual books, and you need to provide this option.

Recommend Products using Affiliate Links

Another way to earn extra income from your books is to

promote affiliate links of products or services you have personally used and found helpful. But be careful not to leave too many links and make your book too spammy. And always be transparent with your readers, which is what I'm going to do right now! I have linked many helpful websites and services in this book, but only certain ones are affiliate links where I will earn a small commission per purchase. And I wouldn't be recommending them only for the fact that they have been instrumental and valuable to me as a writer. All of these products cost the same regardless. Publisher Rocket, KDSPY, Aweber, Grammarly, and the Bose headphones are all affiliate links I recommend. Hotghostwriter is a ghostwriting service I highly recommend, and it does offer a discount. The rest are simply links to useful websites that I have no connection with.

So if you write a book about, say, *fishing*, and you have a particular fishing rod or hook that you love and highly recommend, why not set up an amazon associates account and link the product to your readers? You're promoting Amazon, the seller, and informing your readers of a great product you have experience with. You are essentially advertising these products to an audience for free, so most companies are more willing to allow you to become an affiliate. And sometimes, you're offering discounts the reader won't find elsewhere, so it's a win-win for everyone. For paperbacks, all you have to do is simply insert the links into a free QR code generator site and put the QR image into your book. That's it. Remember to be transparent and don't overdo it, and you're good to go.

Writing More Books and Creating Bundles

Finally, the easiest way to make more money is simply by writing more books. Once you have the first book published, start on your second. The best way to do this is by writing about similar or linked topics. A good strategy is also to write a series of beginner, intermediate, and advanced books on your topic. Also, if you've written multiple books on a subject, be sure to reference those books in your work. Give people a reason to check and buy everything you've written. Once you've written multiple books, you may also want to experiment with selling them as a bundle deal. This is essentially a 2-in-1 bundle, whereby all you have to do is have a freelancer create a new cover combining both original covers for a small price of around $10. Then you simply combine both Ebooks into one and upload it with your new cover. If both Ebooks cost $10 separately to buy, then your bundle deal may cost $15 or $16, which is a better deal for buyers. This creates another stream of income.

Publishing on Audible;

Another way to build your revenue stream is by publishing the audio version of your book. The most popular way to do this is by uploading it onto Audible, which is a subsidiary of Amazon. What you have to realize is that the audiobook industry is growing at a phenomenal rate. Also, this market is still largely untapped - you will have even less competition on this platform.

To do this, you'll have to get your book narrated professionally (depending on what you've written, you can do this yourself). Believe it or not, Audible also offers a narration service. This way, you can have your audiobook professionally narrated and distributed on the platform. Yes, this will cost you, but it's definitely worth it. This is much easier than setting up a microphone in your home. Costs vary from $100 to $250 or more depending on which voice actor you choose and the length of your book. This may seem like another expense but think of the long game! Once uploaded, your audiobook can be sold worldwide on autopilot, and if you have a quality book in a decent niche, you will be well on your way to making that money back. After that, you will be earning pure profit. It's a no-brainer. It's another stream of income you definitely want to avail of.

There's an option to get it done for free. Although if you choose this option, the narrator will take 50% of all royalties from the sales of your audiobook. Depending on your financial situation, you may want to do this, but it's not recommended.

AIA 2.0 – Learn How to Earn 5 Figures a Month Through Audiobooks

Two guys who have made a full program on how to become financially free through selling audiobooks are the Mikkelsen twins. These two young American twins have been on the front of Forbes magazine and became rich from simply selling audiobooks to niche markets. As I've mentioned, the audiobook industry is largely untapped, and people are swaying more and more to the convenience of audiobooks instead of just Ebooks. I highly recommend their content as you will learn a lot about self-publishing Ebooks and audiobooks and how you can make a living from it. Their content and courses go through every step involved in publishing multiple audiobooks and all the tricks and secrets involved in maximizing your sales. Check out their YouTube content and seminars to see if it's something you would be interested in.

How Much Can You Make with Multiple Platforms?

You now know multiple ways of making sales from your book. This income is completely passive, and the various platforms only take a percentage when a purchase is made. If you take the time and effort to create a quality piece of work, it's more than possible to make 30-60 sales per month. As an estimate, that would equate to roughly $200-$600 per month. This is being conservative, and many authors make far more than that. And so, by adding more platforms, you can easily double your sales. Add your audiobook and bundle sales to this, and the sky's the limit.

Once you write multiple books, your income will increase even more. If you produce two high-quality Ebooks in a niche market with high demand and low competition, there is every possibility you could end up making $1,000-$2000 or more per month. Now imagine if you have 3, 4, or even 5 books, and you're selling across multiple platforms along with audiobooks, paperback, and bundle versions. There is a real opportunity to make a high monthly income from this. An income that can potentially exceed anything you could earn at a regular 9-5 job.

CHAPTER 14

Marketing Your Book / Funnels

In the previous chapter, we spoke briefly about selling books on your own website. I want to talk a bit more about this and why it's a real option for people who are serious about becoming Ebook entrepreneurs and want to grow a following online. Maybe you already have a following. (Before we begin, just note that the following advice is mainly for people selling nonfiction books).

It's important that you learn how to market your books online. Uploading your book to Amazon will eventually result in sales, but if you want to take things to the next level, you should also know how to sell yourself. Also, platforms like Amazon can have their drawbacks for authors. They can change rules and royalty percentages anytime they like. Overall, I am a big fan of amazon and highly recommend using the platform. I just wanted to alert you that it is possible to go another route.

So, how do you do this? The simple answer is to set up your own website. Instead of selling your books through Amazon, you sell them through your site and keep the lion's share of the profits. The easiest way to do this is simply by setting up a blog. There is no shortage of online solutions that will allow you to create your own blog. The most popular are WordPress, Wix, and Medium. Again, freelancers on Fiverr can help you set up the website if you need help.

Marketing Techniques for Ebooks:

Whether you are sending visitors to a website you created or to your amazon page, here are the best marketing techniques you can use:

1. Search Engine Optimization (SEO)

SEO is not only for Amazon. It can also be used on Google. The best way to do this is by first creating a list of keywords associated with your book. For example, if you're selling a puppy training guide, you could have keywords like *"how to train your new puppy in 6 easy steps"* or *"beginner's guide to puppy training."* Once this is done, you then create content centered around those keywords. The most common way to do this is simply by adding a blog to your website. You could write blog posts such as *10 ways to train your puppy at home for Busy People.* If everything goes right, you should soon receive visitors to your site. The trick is to not give everything away in your free content and save the most important bits for people who actually buy your book.

2. Social Media

Social media sites are some of the biggest platforms in the world. This means there are millions of potential customers waiting for you. There are endless options for you to utilize the power of social media as a marketing tool. You could start a Twitter account and tweet content related to your niche. There's also the option to join Facebook groups related to your subject or build an author page.

Along with this, you can set up an Instagram account. TikTok is blowing up at the moment with its algorithm allowing people to attain thousands of followers overnight from one good video clip. If your book is related to business or entrepreneurship, don't forget about LinkedIn.

While social media may not suit every author or book, these sites are worth exploring. What's also great about these sites is that they offer a wide variety of advertising options. These options are extremely flexible and can be used to create complex funnels. For example, you could start a Facebook group based on your niche and then advertise that group. From there, you can offer a giveaway and send visitors to your site. It's also possible to advertise your book directly.

3. Amazon Ads for Maximum Profit

Presuming you publish your book on Amazon, Amazon Ads are something you should definitely consider to boost your sales, particularly when you launch your book. Within these ads, you can bid on all the keywords related to your book topic. That way, your book will appear as sponsored product related to the keyword the customer searched. Having strong and consistent optimized ads running will keep your book appearing and ranking in the first search pages of the niche you are in. This will lead to both organic sales and sales from ads.

You can set caps to your ads' daily limit, so it shouldn't cost you too much. And provided your ACOS (advertising cost per sale) is around 40% or lower, you should be ok. Remember, your sales will not be direct profit considering the print costs and the royalty percentage you are in, so monitoring your ACOS and how your ads are performing is very important. It takes a bit of tinkering, but with time you will get the hang of it.

After this, it's all about optimizing your ads, looking at what keywords are profitable and which are not. There are hundreds of different ad strategies and ways to optimize your ads.

Bestselling Book Ads

Thousands of variables can also affect ad performance, and it can be very difficult to tell what works and what doesn't. It can be overwhelming at times. With Ads being such a crucial part of your publishing business, I highly recommend learning more about optimizing ads for maximum profitability. The best course available currently is Best Selling Book Ads which covers every detail and is the most comprehensive, up-to-date Amazon ads course available.

Having watched hundreds of hours of YouTube videos and other courses, this course took my Ads and profitability to the next level. Ivan is an expert in the advertising world. My sales went through the roof once I began implementing the strategies taught. It may seem like a big investment, but if you are serious about becoming a self-publisher for the long term, this is actually amazing value, especially considering the price of other courses. There are 2 levels of the course available, and both are excellent choices. To learn more just scan the QR codes below:

Bestselling Book Ads Essentials:

Bestselling Book Ads Mastery:

4. Videos

Video marketing is enormously powerful. It allows you to build a connection with your audience. Sitting down in front of the camera lets people see who you are and helps to put a face to your name. Another advantage of video is that once you've recorded something, it can be distributed to hundreds of sites. YouTube channels, Instagram, and TikTok, are very popular ways to advertise your work.

5. Q&A Websites

These websites are a great way to connect with people looking for specific information about a topic. They give you a chance to connect with these people, answer their questions, and send visitors to your website (if you're looking for somewhere to get started, www.quora.com is the biggest online Q&A community right now).

6. Ebook Promotion Sites and Services

There are many Ebook promotion sites and services available online. Some websites allow you to upload what's known as an Advanced Readers Copy of your book or an ARC. Pre-readers get your book for free and will leave a review. When your book is live, you can then ask those readers to post their reviews, giving your book credibility, which is hugely important.

Aside from that, there are many free and paid services that will promote your book to their audiences online. Amazon also has a feature called KDP select, whereby you can offer your book for free for a few days. This will help get your book ranking on Amazon.

7. Offline Advertising

Don't forget about offline advertising. The simplest way to sell your book is simply by advertising it in places like magazines and newspapers. While this can be expensive, the results are phenomenal if done right. One of the cheapest forms of offline advertising is classified ads. Many specialist magazines carry these ads.

A good example is the Fortean Times. Anyone who has read this magazine will know the classified ads section is literally stuffed with advertisements for all kinds of books. You may also want to consider running classified ads in your local newspaper.

8. Speaking Engagements

Public speaking can be a wonderful form of marketing for your book. It helps to position you as the expert in your field and can generate visitors to your website or actual book sales. While this method is slightly trickier than other things we've mentioned, it's worth looking into.

9. Book Reviews

Book reviews are the go-to marketing tool for traditional publishers. Most magazines and newspapers have a section devoted to reviewing books. If you're self-publishing, getting your book into these sections may be difficult. The next best option is the internet. There are hundreds of bloggers and website owners who may be willing to review your book. You should also look at BookTube. This word refers to people who run YouTube channels devoted to books. Many of these channels have hundreds of thousands of subscribers, and being mentioned by them can dramatically boost your book sales.

10. Bundles and Deals

Always consider ways to bundle your books and sell them as a package. This becomes possible once you've written more than one book. As we discussed earlier, you can then be in a position to offer a 2-in-1 bundle deal or sell your books as part of a series. Something else you should do is hold sales from time to time. Any holiday or special occasion can be an excuse for a sale. Christmas, New Year, Valentine's Day (which is especially effective if you're selling romance novels), your birthday, or any other date are all days on which you can hold sales.

Using Marketing Funnels to Sell your Book

Another advanced way to market your books is with a marketing funnel. This is a term for follow-up marketing. It describes the process whereby you capture the details of your visitors and then follow up with them later. While building a marketing funnel can be extremely complex, the simplest version works like this.

1. Drive Traffic

The first step in your marketing funnel is getting people to visit your website. This is usually done with one of the marketing techniques we mentioned above.

2. Send Visitors to a Landing Page

These visitors are sent to a special page on your website called a landing page. This can either be the homepage of your site or a special landing page site you have created for this purpose. These pages are not too difficult to set up. You certainly don't have to be an expert at building websites to create one.

3. You offer them a "Lead Magnet."

When people land on this page, you offer them what's known as a lead magnet. This is essentially a gift which you give to visitors for their contact details. Most often, this will be their email address (you may have already seen these offers all over the internet). All they must do is enter their email address, and you will allow them to download the gift for free. Your lead magnet can be a sample of your book, but it may also be something to do with your niche. For example, if your book is about running a marathon, you can create a lead magnet titled *How to buy running shoes that last*. If you're a fiction writer, you can give them a free book or maybe a short story.

4. Follow up Email

Once you have their email address, start with follow-up marketing. This will involve sending emails to your prospective customers. To do this (and capture email addresses), you'll need to sign up for something called an "autoresponder." This is an online software program that sends out emails. While this may sound complicated, these tools are relatively easy to use. There are many free autoresponders available online, and also paid versions.

The best of these, in my opinion, is **Aweber**, which I highly recommend.

Here is QR code:

5. Send them to your Sales Page

When sending out emails, you will use some type of copywriting that is meant to entice them into buying your book. The whole next chapter, *The Art of Copywriting*, is dedicated to learning this craft. At the bottom of these emails, you insert a link to a sales page. This is a page where you try to sell them your book, but it can also be your Amazon page. Just make sure your emails are short, to the point, and valuable! Don't make your emails spammy, and don't send too many. I believe one email a week is the sweet spot. These four steps make up your most basic marketing funnel. While things can get a bit more complicated, these are the most often-used steps.

The reason marketing funnels are so powerful is that most people rarely buy products on their first encounter. They often need some time to warm up first and may only buy weeks or months after discovering the product. Moreover, most people will only buy something once they know, like, and trust the person selling it. With follow-up marketing, you can achieve these aims. You stay in touch with the person and this gives you a chance to develop a relationship with them. They get to know you and also learn about your product.

Consider the alternative where someone visits your website and leaves after 30 seconds or a minute. In this case, it's highly unlikely that you will ever see that person again. This means you may have lost a potential sale. But by offering a gift and capturing their details, you improve the chances of that person becoming a customer. This is the primary reason marketing funnels are so powerful and widely used. And the following bonus chapter will help you develop the skill of copywriting. After that, you will have all the tools to start writing, publishing, and marketing your first Ebook.

CHAPTER 15

Mastering The Art of Copywriting

"Disclaimer: in this bonus chapter, you will learn all the tips and tricks involved in copywriting and how attention-grabbing headlines and adverts can draw customers in. You may not agree with some of the material in this chapter. I certainly don't. Some of it may come across as manipulative or over the top. Just remember that every top company in the world uses these techniques in some form. Every day on social media or through email, you get bombarded with advertisements, clickbait articles, and sales pitches. So, understanding how this works is going to help you not be as easily led in the future. But it will also greatly assist you with your self-publishing journey."

To become a successful Ebook publisher, the writing aspect is only about 50% of the success story. Marketing your books makes up the remaining 50% of this business. Yes, having a high-quality book written is crucial. But if you don't know how to market it correctly, it simply won't sell that well. Similarly, the opposite is true. With good marketing of a low-quality book, it will sell in the beginning, but bad reviews may affect you in the long run. Take this chapter for what it is, and use elements of it in your advertising without overdoing it. Because the bottom line is that to make consistent sales, you have to learn how to write effective advertising copy, and that's what we're going to talk about in this chapter.

What is Copywriting?

To put it simply, copywriting is essentially the art and science of writing marketing text. It could also be described as the art of writing adverts. An even simpler way to describe copywriting - it's words that sell. For example, let's say you want to sell a special kind of widget. To do this, you'll obviously have to market the product. So, you'll need to create advertising - and the words used in those adverts are known as copy, and writing those words is copywriting (And the people who write those words are known as *copywriters*).

Copy for Your Book Description Page

Why is this so important? Because good copywriting can often mean the difference between the success and failure of your book. Suppose you don't have excellent copy written on your Amazon description or advertisement. In that case, chances are you are missing out on potential sales from customers who are on the fence, from customers who clicked into your book but didn't like the description. Now, some of you may disagree with this. Yes, it is still possible to sell books with no marketing or advertising (this will usually depend on how badly people want your book). But good marketing can mean the difference between selling dozens or hundreds of books.

What it really comes down to is how successful you want to be. If you're content with just getting by, then fine. You don't have to study copywriting. But if you're someone who wants to be ultra-successful - if you want to do this as a full-time job - then this stuff is essential. And in many cases, you don't have a choice. If you've written a book and you're not making sales, then the only way to remedy this is through physically *selling* the book, and to do that, you'll need to learn copywriting. This is why copywriting is such a valuable skill because it can create money on demand.

Another reason you should learn this highly valuable skill is that it opens up another revenue stream, i.e., you can become a freelance copywriter. After all, if you've created highly lucrative marketing funnels for your own book, other people will be more than happy to pay you to do the same for them. Now, this may all sound like an exaggeration. But this skill alone can help companies double their sales or more. It's a skill that's worth a lot of money in itself.

Now, let's say you've created an Amazon listing for your book and…

- You don't give people a reason to buy the product.
- You don't appeal to their deepest wants and needs.
- You don't handle their objections.
- You don't describe the features of that product and how they benefit the customer.
- You don't provide proof to back up your claims.

You cannot grab their attention from the very first word and keep them reading to the end. If you do all the above, guess what happens? Nothing! That's right. In this case, you probably won't sell many copies of your book. Alternatively, if you do these things and more, the sky's the limit. Therefore, copy is essential. It's a skill that can be developed over time, and it's something you can learn too. It's going to benefit both your writing and your marketing skills.

Understanding the Product
When writing copy, the very first step is understanding your product. You need to have a firm grasp of the features, benefits, and advantages of what you're selling. What does the product do for your prospect? How can it help improve their lives and achieve their goals faster and easier? The simplest way to do this is by drawing up a list of features in your product. For example, let's say you're selling a car, and the basic features include:

1. It gets 40 miles per gallon.
2. It has an anti-rust coating.
3. It's crash tested.
4. It has 250 horsepower.
5. And so on…

Think about all the features your product contains and write them down. You need to go through your book, line by line, and pull out every feature. Next, you want to turn these features into benefits. Remember, prospects are primarily concerned about the benefits associated with buying your product. They don't necessarily care about the color, size, or shape of what you're selling. They are primarily interested in what your product can do for them. How can it help them learn a new skill, save and make money, get healthy, meet their soulmate, or otherwise live a better life? Looking at the above list, these features can be turned into the following benefits:

1. It saves you money. This means transportation is cheaper.
2. The car will last longer. It won't rust, and your car will hold its value when it comes time to sell.
3. The car is safer. Because crash tested, safety measures and adjustments would have been made at the time of its production.
4. The car is super-fast. It can accelerate quickly and get you out of potentially dangerous situations. You can also reach destinations faster. And you have 250 horsepower!

To summarize this process, you want to inspect your product and list every feature. Then think about what those features do for the prospect and turn them into benefits, one by one.

Understanding the Customer

Next, you need to understand the customer, which is even more important than understanding the product. The reason is that you absolutely must know whom you are selling to on a very deep level. You need to understand the market like the back of your hand. In fact, you need to know these people better than you know yourself. You must do this to the point where you can almost read their minds. This includes knowing things like their fears, beliefs, what they have tried before, what they believe about products like yours, what keeps them awake at night, and their dreams, wishes, hopes, and goals.

Bottom line, as we've mentioned before, customer research is vital. You must know what your prospective customers actually want. Once you know what they want, you can then give it to them. If you don't know what they are looking for, you may end up trying to sell a product that they are not interested in.

In chapter 5, we spoke about "joining the conversation that is going on inside their heads." What this means is that they are thinking a certain way about the problems in their lives. By repeating what they are thinking back to them, you will connect with them on a deep level and help them understand that your product is the best solution to their problem. The only way to do this is with research. You need to read everything you can that has to do with your market. It also helps to consume the products your market is buying. For example, if you're selling a book about yoga, go out and buy as many yoga books and videos as possible. Look for commonalities in these products. Pay attention to the copy they use to sell the product and anything else which stands out. This should give you a good indication of what works in the market.

It also helps to put yourself in their shoes and try to become a part of the market if you are not already. For example, I'm assuming if you are writing a yoga book, you most likely already do yoga and have some interest in it, but if you don't and it's still something you want to write about, then you need to sign up for some classes. We talked about writing books on topics you are familiar with and experienced with, but if you are writing something new to you, it's definitely advised to get some real-life experience in that topic, whatever it may be.

Market research can be challenging. In the past, you would have to do customer surveys and interviews. You would have to find people in your market in real life and talk to them. Today we have the internet, which makes everything so much easier. The internet gives you the ability to know exactly what prospects in your market are thinking. For example, there are hundreds of forums, websites, and Facebook pages devoted to every topic under the sun.

Let's say you're selling a healthy diet book. All you have to do is go to Facebook and search for keywords related to your market. This will give you dozens of results. From there, you can read through the pages and groups that come up and see how the people in your market think, feel, and act. What you're looking for is called "hot phrases." These are specific phrases you can insert into your copy.

Let's say you go onto a website and see something like this: "I want to drop a jean size." Being able to drop a size in your clothes is a goal that many people have. They may have been a smaller size before and remember what that felt like, so they use that as the benchmark when they are trying to create a healthier diet and lifestyle. So if you have a proven product that has helped people drop a jean size in the past, you can use this phrase in your copy to help you sell that product.

Ultimately, market research is about becoming a "sales detective" and investigating the market on a deep level, finding out the needs and desires of the target market. Do this correctly, and you will massively boost the selling power of your copy.

Anatomy of Great Copy

Writing copy is just like playing music. What I mean by this is that all great copy has a specific structure, just like all songs have a structure. There are certain musical rules and theories. When you follow these, you produce great music. If you violate these rules, all you create is discordant noise.

For this reason, it's crucial that you structure your copy correctly. There are literally hundreds of ways to do this. One of the most famous is **AIDA**. It stands for **A**ttention, **I**nterest, **D**esire, and **A**ction. This is not necessarily for book descriptions but more for emails and advertisements. Here's how it works:

1. **Attention** – start by grabbing the prospect's attention with a powerful headline and opening statement.
2. **Interest** – say something which interests them. Give them a reason for reading the copy and tell them about the benefits they will get from using your product.
3. **Desire** – next, create desire. In this part, you list more benefits of your product and what they can get from buying or using it. You want to fan the flames of their desire to the point where they feel it's impossible not to buy your book.
4. **Action** – when this is done, it's now time to take action. Tell them how they can get the product and how much it costs. Create a sense of urgency and get them to act quickly.

If the prospect hesitates, there's a good chance they will forget about your book, and then you've lost the sale. There are many ways to create urgency. For example:

1. You can mention that there are only so many physical copies left (i.e., only 15 copies left in stock, order now)
2. Offer a discount for responding immediately (i.e., order in the next hour and receive a $10 discount).

3. Offer a free bonus for buying the product now (i.e., order today, and you'll get this bonus guide FREE).

The AIDA structure is a very simple formula that is really only used by beginners. There are other advanced ways to structure your copy. One of the most popular is the Perry Belcher 12-step sales letter.

In case you don't know, Perry Belcher is an internet marketer who made millions by selling supplements online. He claims to have created a sales letter structure that was immensely powerful and extremely effective. The structure of this sales letter goes like this:

1. **Call out to your Audience** – address your target audience and say something which speaks directly to them, i.e., "tired of unrealistic weight-loss diets that don't last?"

2. **Get their Attention** – write an attention-grabbing headline, i.e., "Here's how to lose 10 pounds in 2 weeks without any ridiculous dieting".

3. **Back up your Headline with a Sub-Headline which explains what you meant** – briefly explain the headline, i.e., "Now you can lose weight without starving yourself or giving up your favorite foods."

4. **Identify the Problem** – talk about the specific problem, struggle, or challenge the audience has, i.e., "So you want to get healthy without giving up your favorite meals?".

5. **Provide the Solution** – reveal your product as the solution to whatever problem they have. Explain why it's the best option for solving their problem, i.e., "This simple healthy diet tip can take away 90% of food cravings".

6. **Show Pain and Cost of Development** – talk about how difficult it was to develop your product or solution, i.e., "It took over 10 years of trials and testing to finally come up with this realistic healthy diet plan".

7. **Explain Ease of Use** – show how easy it is to use your solution, i.e., "All you have to do is follow the 6 simple steps in this plan".

8. **Show Speed of Results** – give them a time frame in which they can expect to see results, i.e., "In just 2 weeks, you can potentially lose as much as 10 pounds".

9. **Future Cast** – tell them how great the future will be once they have solved this problem, i.e., "Imagine getting down to your old jean or shirt size, and how would that feel?"

10. **Tell them about the Benefits of your product** – use bullet points to list the benefits of your program.

11. **Get Social Proof** – include real testimonials from satisfied buyers once your product or program has

been tested. This helps to demonstrate the effectiveness of your product.

12. **Make the Offer** – tell them exactly what they are getting and how much it costs.

13. **Add Bonuses** – if your product comes with any bonuses, then tell them about these.

14. **Build up your Value** – tell them how much the product is worth and why the price you are asking is justified.

15. **Reveal your Price** – Reveal the price of your product which should seem far lower than expected given the value it will provide.

16. **Make a Guarantee** – if you are using a guarantee, then talk about it. It's recommended that you add a guarantee, as this is also a great way to boost sales.

17. **Call to Action** – be specific and tell them exactly how to order your product.

18. **Give a Warning** – tell them what's going to happen if they don't buy, i.e., the price will be going back up very soon to its correct value.

19. **Close with a Reminder** – go over the above steps and summarize them at the end of your sales letter.

Crafting Your Headline for Your Description

The best way to come up with a headline is to simply use

what has already worked as a guide and change it to your own unique style. Take a look at existing headlines and modify them for your products. Most great copywriters do this as it is highly effective.

What you should do is start putting together a swipe file of headlines. In case you don't know, a swipe file is basically a collection of adverts. Copywriters use it for inspiration, motivation, and as study material. Anytime you see a great advert or piece of copy, save it and add it to your collection. Swipe files are also important when learning how to write copy. Ideally, you should spend some time every week reading through your swipe file and studying the adverts. Over time, this will help to make you a better copywriter. That being said, don't copy and paste blindly. Always use your head when adapting copy for your own products.

Now, there are some rules to follow when crafting your headline.

1. **Keep Your Headlines Short** – most people try to do too much in their headlines. They write headlines that are 10, 20, or even 30 words long and jam as much into them as possible. This is a bad idea. Remember, the purpose of your headline is to get the prospect's attention. For this reason, it should be short, sweet, and to the point.

2. **Headlines Need to be Punchy** – your headline needs to grab readers by the eyeballs and refuse to let go. The way you do this is by using the most

powerful words possible. Remember, some words are more visceral than others. Don't use the word kill. Say slaughter instead. Don't talk about breaking something - rupture, fracture, shatter, or smash are far better alternatives. Consider how the words make your readers feel and the deeper meaning behind them.

3. **Headlines Must be Credible** – people need to believe what you say in your headline. You also need to establish the credibility of the person who is talking to them. This gives them a reason to believe your claims. For example, let's say you're selling a weightlifting training program, and within the program is a unique tip that a former bodybuilding world champion adapted to his own training. You could say something like, "Bodybuilding world champion reveals what most people will NEVER understand about weight training." This type of headline establishes the credibility of the message which follows.

4. **Give Them a Benefit for Reading** – you don't always have to do this, but your headline should imply a benefit to reading the copy. An easy way to do this is to imply that the reader will learn something from the copy. For example, you could say something like, "3 tricks to passing exams that they didn't teach you in school". Just note that if you're going to do this, it's vital that you use the

benefits which your target market most deeply desires.

5. **Use Curiosity Whenever you can** – the easiest way to improve your headlines is by using curiosity. Wherever you can, introduce the element of curiosity. This goes hand in hand with the above point. Start by listing a benefit in your headline. Then make them curious about how they can gain this benefit by reading the copy or purchasing your product.

6. **Use Simple Questions** – one of the easiest ways to write a headline is by asking a simple question. Ideally, this should be a question that your market is already asking or something they are desperate to know the answer to. The questions you ask should make them curious enough to read your copy. For example, you could say, "Is it possible to get perfect meditation in 2 weeks with no experience?" This type of headline makes them wonder what the answer is and naturally, they will continue to read your copy.

Writing great headlines takes practice. When writing copy for your book, the best thing you can do is write lots of headlines. This might sound like overkill, but you should write at least 20 or 30 headlines. Do this, and you're bound to find something that works.

Crafting Openings

Besides your headline, the opening is the most important element of your copy. This is because your first sentence gets them to read the second sentence and so on all the way to the end of the copy where – if you've done your job right – they will order the book. The first few lines of your copy should give them a reason for reading. Most often, this will be some benefit or something that makes them curious. The essential rule is that you need to grab their attention immediately and give them a reason to continue reading.

Here are 4 things you must do when crafting your opening:

1. **Expand upon your Headline** – the first lines of your opening should say more about your headline. Remember, you want to keep your headline short. This means you'll have plenty of room to expand things. When doing this, you want to explain exactly what you meant in the headline. You also want to give them a compelling reason to carry on reading the rest of the copy.

2. **Trigger their Curiosity** – you need to make them curious enough to read the rest of the copy. The way to do this is by promising to reveal amazing benefits. Tell them exactly what they are going to learn and discover by reading your copy and get them curious enough to continue.

3. **Introduce your Benefits** – this is probably the most important part of the opening. You need to clearly list the benefits of your product. What are they going to get or learn? What is the product going to do for them?

4. **Make it Easy to read** – the opening of your sales copy should be short, simple, and easy to read. It should take almost zero effort to skim through. Use brief sentences, paragraphs, and bullets (bullets are especially powerful in your opening).

One of the best things to do when learning copywriting is to study Reader's Digest. This is one of the world's most popular and best-selling magazines. There's a good reason for this: the quality of their articles and headlines is way above average. If you're serious about improving your copy skills, I recommend you start buying this magazine or check out the articles online on their website, <u>Readers Digest</u>. Read these articles and study the headlines they use in their articles. Also, examine the first few sentences of the articles, and observe how they pull you into the article. Remember, the goal of the first sentence is to get you curious enough to read the rest of the article.

Using Open Loops

One of the most powerful copywriting methods is the open loop. This is essentially a psychological technique for creating curiosity and forcing people to read your copy.

Let me explain: Pretend you're talking with a friend. They're telling you some juicy piece of gossip. You're paying attention because what they're saying is very interesting. You're in a state of suspense. You need to know what happens next. Then suddenly, the doorbell rings. It's their sister, she comes in, and the conversation changes. But guess what? You're still desperate for them to finish the story. You must know how it ends. Eventually, their sister leaves. At this point, what's the first thing you'll do? It's obvious. You'll ask them to finish the story! This is basically an open loop. It's a technique used everywhere, from books to movies, especially on TV. A great example of open loops is cliffhangers. A TV show will end on a massive cliffhanger, and of course, you watch the next episode to find out what happens.

Using Bullet Points

One of the most powerful and often used copywriting techniques is bullets (i.e., bullet points). These are bite-sized pieces of copy that are scattered throughout the text. They   look   like   this:

- Bullet 1…
- Bullet 2…
- Bullet 3…
- Bullet 4…
- Bullet 5…
- etc.

Bullets serve two purposes. The first is to break the text up and make it easier to read. When the text is broken up into bullets, it becomes far easier to skim through. Bullets also keep people reading. You read the first bullet and go onto the next one and the next, and so on. Bullets essentially allow people to quickly scan through the copy and get the information they need.

The big secret is that someone will often buy your product simply because of a single bullet. Quite often, there will be one bullet that arouses such incredible curiosity that the prospect will buy the product right there and then simply because they have to know what you're talking about. This is the true power of bullets, and it's why they are so important.

There are two types of bullets: blind bullets and open bullets. Blind bullets are where you tease them with something. You hint at a secret without revealing it. Open bullets are where you tell them directly about the benefits of your product, i.e., 7 powerful muscle-building secrets that only personal trainers know about.

The way to write bullets is to study great copy. You need to start building your swipe file and see what other copywriters are doing. This is really the only way to learn the art of bullet writing. But to get you started, here are a few basic formulas for writing bullets. These are 20 proven bullet writing techniques that are used by some of the best writers in the business:

1. The **How-To** bullet – this is by far the most common form of bullet. You've probably noticed it all over the internet. There's almost nothing to explain here. Simply combine the words how to

with something people want to know about. For example, "How to make $200 per day with tiny little classified ads?"

2. The **Secret-To** bullet – this works well when you have a piece of information that isn't common knowledge. This way, you can justify the use of the word secret. Usually, the secret will have something to do with how your prospect will get the benefit. This bullet also works well when combined with the phrase "Little-known...". For example, "The little-known secrets to writing irresistible bullets."

3. The **Why** bullet – this bullet is great for building curiosity. You're essentially promising to reveal why something is a certain way. The idea behind this is that knowing the why will help to improve the prospect's life. For example, "Why you should write short headlines."

4. The **What** bullet – these bullets serve two purposes. First, they can give prospects specific instructions (i.e., "What you need to do now to gain muscle"). They can also share specific information and arouse curiosity (i.e., "What personal trainers never tell you about weight training")

5. The **What Never** bullet – this is a variation on the what bullet. The power of this bullet is that it creates curiosity. You're promising to tell them

about a mistake they've been making. For example, "What never to eat if you want to avoid bloating." You can also use the phrases, "Why you should not..." or "What to avoid...".

6. The **PLUS** bullet – this bullet creates greed by promising the reader more. These bullets work best when used at the end of a list of bullets, i.e., "PLUS: 10 more ways to end food cravings".

7. The **Number** bullet – this is another bullet you see everywhere online. Simply group things together and present them as a bullet. This can be important information or ways of doing something. For example, "10 foods which cause indigestion and what you should eat instead".

8. The **Right-Wrong** bullet – this bullet uses the reader's assumptions against them. You start by bringing up a commonly believed idea and then debunk it. This works because people often want to know when they are wrong – especially about things that are important to them, i.e., "Long headlines work best, right? Wrong! Here's why shorter headlines are better".

9. The **Warning** bullet – this is a great bullet for warning prospects about anything which may be a danger to them. This type of bullet is also great for targeting any fears your prospect may have. It

works well if you follow it up with a solution to the danger you are warning them about. For example, "WARNING: Doctors agree the overuse of earphones can cause hearing loss… Here's how to prevent yourself from becoming a victim." With this bullet, you can also use the phrases CAUTION or ATTENTION.

10. The **Are You** bullet – here you ask the prospect about something they are probably already doing. You then offer them specific advice or information. i.e., "Are you making the same silly mistakes when dieting?"

11. The **Gimmick** bullet – with this bullet, you take a technique or piece of information from your product and give it a name. This works best if you're selling books because it helps to create curiosity about what's inside them. When using this bullet, pick an unusual name. You can also choose the name of an area or something famous. For example, "The Hollywood technique for writing bullets" or "The Scandinavian diet secret, which almost no one knows about."

12. The **Statement of Interest plus Benefit** bullet – this works best when you have an interesting piece of information that you can combine with a powerful benefit. It also works great when mixed with a "How" or "Why" bullet. For example,

"Drowning is the 3rd leading cause of accidental death. But did you know it's possible to save a drowning person even if you can't swim?"

13. The **Direct Benefit** bullet – in this bullet, you simply state your benefit. You want to phrase it using an action verb. For example, "Build a ton of muscle mass by only doing 3 workouts a week!"

14. The **Specific Question** bullet – as we've mentioned before, questions are a great way to draw readers into your copy. To use this bullet, simply ask an intriguing question. Your question should be something that is important to the market. For example, "What is the most powerful word you can use when writing copy? The answer may surprise you!"

15. The **if-Then** bullet – this is probably the simplest bullet formula. The *if* helps to engage your readers. And the *then* creates curiosity, i.e., "If you want to stop your divorce, then here's what you need to do NOW."

16. The **When** bullet – this is great if you want to promise a benefit in a specific time frame. You're saying to do something at a particular time, and you'll get this result. It naturally makes people curious because they'll want to know when they need to do the thing to get the benefit, i.e., "What

time of the day you should exercise to ensure maximum muscle gain."

17. The **Quickest-Easiest** bullet – when you're stating there is a quicker, easier way to do something or achieve some result. This bullet works because people always want to get things easier, faster, and with less effort. For example, "The quickest, easiest way to write world-class copy."

18. The **Truth** bullet – this works well when there is some controversy in your market. It's also good when there is conflicting or confusing information, or people aren't sure about something, i.e., "The TRUTH about poor posture and how to get rid of it for good."

19. The **Better** bullet – this can be used when something is good, but you have a better alternative. You can also use the word "Beyond." For example, "Better than squats! This exercise is easier and builds stronger quads faster" or, "Beyond dieting! Here's a better alternative to starving yourself".

20. The **Single** bullet – this bullet is best used when you have a powerful piece of information or a benefit that exceeds everything else. It works because you're promising to give the prospect

something incredible that could potentially change their life. For example, "The single most powerful money-making secret."

Something else you can do is mix and match different types of bullets. This works particularly well. Just remember that the most important thing is always <u>curiosity</u>. It's almost the same as an open loop, making the reader desperate to find out the answer. It's also a good idea to consult your swipe file. As we've said, when learning how to write copy, it's important that you build up a swipe file and then study it as often as you can. Consult the adverts you have collected and study any bullets you find. Pay attention to how they are written, and then use what you've learned when writing your own copy.

Another great way to learn bullet writing is by using the internet. Clickbait headlines are essentially bullets. They are designed to trigger your curiosity and make you click on the article. Start visiting websites like <u>BuzzFeed</u> and study the headlines they use. <u>The Daily Mail</u> also has great headlines and bullet points. I don't recommend making your copy for a book too *clickbaity,* but examining clickbait will certainly assist you.

Using Emotional Motivators

What you need to realize is that most of the choices we make are based on our <u>emotions</u>. People do not think logically when making buying decisions. Their choices are mostly based on how they feel. What this means is that, to get them to purchase your product, you need to learn how to influence their emotions using words.

So how do you do this? Essentially you use something known as the dominant emotion in your market. What this basically means is that in your marketplace, there will be one emotion that is stronger than others. This could be anger, fear, desire, joy, frustration, pain, or some other emotion. You need to research the marketplace and discover the most powerful emotion your prospects feel about their problem or issue. You then need to write copy that evokes this emotion in the reader. Doing this allows you to bond with them and is also a powerful sales motivator.

Here's an example of this in action:

Imagine you want to buy a new hybrid car. You're sick to death of rising gas prices and need to save money. One day you decide to go down to the dealership. A salesperson approaches you and introduces himself. You tell him you want a hybrid car, so he starts talking about the incredible deals he has, his financing plan, how great the car is, and so on. Then he shows you the car and starts talking about all its wonderful features, benefits, and so on.

What do you think would happen in this scenario? What would be your gut feeling about this car? Would you feel excited to buy it? You probably wouldn't feel anything. Yes, you want to buy a car, and his car seems like a good deal. But of course, it's going to sound like a good deal, that's his job, and he probably earns a commission off each sale. For these reasons, you will still have an inner resistance to buying the car and are unlikely to purchase it.

Now imagine a second scenario. You walk into another dealership and meet a second salesperson. But instead of talking about the car, he talks about you! He mentions how expensive gas is and how prices are supposed to rise even further. He also mentions that gas prices will sometimes go up even when oil prices have gone down.

Next, he starts talking about how much money people spend on gas and how that money could be saved and used for other things. You both begin to discuss the topic. The car isn't even mentioned yet. What do you think would happen in this scenario? You'd probably develop a powerful bond with this salesperson. You'd begin to like and trust this person on a deep level. Not only that, you'd feel angry at a gut level. Anger at the gas companies, oil companies, the government, and the fact that you have to waste your hard-earned money on gas. Money you could be spending on other things like your children's education, going on holiday, or repairing your home.

Now, here's the important part: which salesperson would you rather buy a new car from? The answer is most likely - salesperson #2. Instead of starting off telling you about the features and benefits of the car, salesperson #2 started with a strong, attention-grabbing statement that's filled with emotion. Not only that, they took the time to learn and discover exactly how you're feeling about the topic – instead of simply trying to sell you a product. Another reason this approach works so well is that it doesn't initially feel as if salesperson #2 is trying to sell you something. This allows you to circumvent the resistance that people usually feel toward sales messages.

Good Guy vs Bad Boy

Here is another way to think of it. Why is it that the good guy can have everything – a nice car, millions in the bank, education, and good looks… but… some women still go for the bad boy with dirty clothes, a bad attitude, and no money. The reason is simple. The bad boy makes women *feel* something. He triggers their emotions. The bad boy is exciting. He's dangerous and connects with her on a deep level. Meanwhile, the "perfect guy" is nice and conservative but doesn't make her feel anything.

I'm not saying you should leave out features and benefits in your copy. But what you have to do is use emotions. Write in a way that triggers the reader's dominant emotion - whether that is desire, fear, frustration, or something else.

Finally, don't forget that the easiest way to influence your readers' emotions is by deeply understanding your market. Know the most pressing issues which are present in your market. What do they most secretly desire? What keeps them up at night, what are they afraid of, and what motivates them to take action? Once you know these things, you can simply feed them back to your readers and build a powerful rapport with them.

<u>Building Your Swipe File</u>

Throughout this chapter, I've mentioned the importance of building a swipe file. This is something every copywriter does, and it's a must-have resource. A swipe file has many uses.

For example:

- It can be a source of headlines and other pieces of copy, such as opening lines, closing statements, and bullets which can be modified, adapted and used in your own promotions.
- It can help you learn about the market you're selling to. Let's say you're selling a protein supplement product. By studying weight training adverts in your swipe file, you learn about the desires, fears, and motivations of your market. You can learn what type of benefits and products they respond to. This is one of the most valuable ways to use your swipe file.
- The adverts in your swipe file can also be a source of inspiration if you're still struggling when writing your copy.
- Swipe files are also used as a general study tool when learning how to write copy.

More Tips for Writing Great Copy

Here are some other tips that will help you improve your copy further and become a better writer. They will also help you polish and perfect your copy over time.

1. Vary Your Sentence Lengths.

When writing copy, your sentences should be short and sweet. Short sentences are easier to read. Therefore, they keep the prospect reading all the way to the end of your copy. Short sentences also help the copy flow better. That being said, you should vary your sentence length. You want to mix short and long sentences together to avoid monotony.

At the same time, you want to also vary your paragraph lengths. Shorter paragraphs are easier to read and keep the prospect going. Longer paragraphs can be used when explaining technical details about your product or giving the reader important information.

You can also use punctuation to vary copy. Something which works well is dashes – they can break up long sentences. Another punctuation device that works well is colons. For example: when you use a colon, people will generally read what comes after it. You can also **bold** certain words, <u>underline</u> others, and use CAPITALS or *italics*.

2. Use Powerful and Sensory Words.

If you're going to be a copywriter, then you need to expand your vocabulary and start using *power* words and phrases. The fact is that some words and phrases are more powerful than others. For example, look at the following:

- White-hot
- Wickedly effective
- Disgusting
- Get away with
- House of cards
- Greedy
- Priceless

These are all examples of *power* words and phrases. They make your copy more compelling and colorful. You should start building up a list of any power words and phrases you stumble across. Also, look through your swipe file to find examples of these words and phrases.

Another thing you can do is employ figures of speech. These make your copy easier to read and allow you to convey more information in fewer words. Figures of speech include things like:

- Time flies when you're having fun
- Slipped through your fingers
- Pain in the neck
- It takes two to tango
- Keep your nose to the grindstone

Something else you should use is what's known as bucket brigade phrases (also known as transition phrases). These are short brief sentences that are used to transition between paragraphs. They are also used to move smoothly from sentence to sentence and keep people reading. Here are some examples of bucket brigade phrases:

- And here's more good news
- But wait – there's more
- BTW, one more thing
- Can you imagine that
- In addition to
- Here's the deal
- Just imagine

- Listen
- Now, this may surprise you
- Let's face it
- Not only that
- In fact
- One more thing

3. Read your copy OUT LOUD.

This is an old-school technique for polishing your copy. Once the copy is 100% finished, read it out loud at least 5-10 times. Doing this will help the copy read and flow more naturally. It's also a great way to proofread your work and will help you spot mistakes and things that need to be corrected or changed.

4. Write at a Fourth-Grade Level.

In writing, there is the popular Flesch-Kincaid scale, which we mentioned before. This is a way of analyzing writing to determine how easy it is to read. If you use short, simple sentences and words, then the scale will be a higher number and the text easier to read.

The scale is scored out of 100. For example, a score of 90-100 means your text is pretty easy to read and can be understood by anyone. A score of 50 or lower means the text is difficult to read and will only be understood by university graduates.

Unfortunately, a lot of people in the world do not read and actually struggle to read. This means that your text should always be as simple as possible. Any copy you write should score at least 80 on this scale. Doing this helps your copy appeal to the broadest range of people possible. Just search for the Flesch-Kincaid scale, and you will find plenty of tools for grading your writing. (I recommend you use <u>this one</u>).

5. Start Writing Out Adverts.

The best way to get good at copywriting is not rocket science. All great copywriters use this technique, but it's something many people don't like to do. The reason is that it's hard work and takes time. That being said, if you're willing to put in the effort, it can help to dramatically improve your skills. The technique is to simply write out – by hand – great adverts.

There are a few reasons this technique is so powerful. The first is that it creates a neurological imprint inside your mind. By writing out the copy, you are basically programming your subconscious mind with the techniques of writing great copy.

The second is that it allows you to see "under the hood," so to speak. By writing the copy out, you gain a far deeper understanding of what's going on and how the copy is constructed.

Yes, many don't enjoy doing this because, as we said, it's difficult. But you should at least try it. Write out two or three adverts for any type of product or use your book ideas and see if it makes a difference in how you write copy. If you see an ad in a newspaper or magazine for a new TV or washing machine, write out an exaggerated, better version of that advert and get creative. It can be a fun exercise, and will help you improve your copy.

Finally, the best way to get good at writing copy is with practice. Writing copy is like everything else in life - the more you practice, the better you'll get. The most important thing is to reach the point where you've written copy that converts into sales. This is the ultimate test of your copywriting skills and is what really takes you from beginner to advanced. It's not enough to know how to write copy. After all, copywriting isn't just creative writing. It's not just about coming up with pretty sentences – it's also about selling your books and products you've worked so hard on.

As I said at the beginning of this chapter, take this content with a pinch of salt. While it was important to dive deep into this topic, do not become spammy and distasteful with your copy. Once your book is high-quality, offers genuine value, and you have good copy written to persuade potential buyers to purchase, all will be well. They will be glad they bought your book and may leave a positive review.

CHAPTER 16

How to Write Your Ebook in 7 Simple Steps

This section will briefly recap the 7 steps needed to write and sell your Ebook. These points will help to summarize what you've learned so far and give you a checklist to work through.

1. Brainstorm Idea / Data Research / Decide

Get a sheet of paper out and brainstorm all the book ideas you think you could write about. Write them down. Think of your unique talents and experiences. Think about something you have learned that you can pass knowledge on to. Think about a certain topic that you wish there was a book about. Write them all down. If you cannot think of anything good, then do some research on the internet to find some good niches or modern-day topics worth exploring and go from there.

Next, you want to input your book idea keywords in **KDSPY** to check if these niches are profitable. This amazing tool will show you the top books for that keyword search and their **BSR** (best sellers rank). If the average of all the books is below 200,000, then you are on to a winner. High demand has been established.

Next, if you want to check what the competition is like and how many searches are being made for these books. If below 9000, the competition is not very high. Below 5000 is even more ideal.

To check for any related keywords and see how many searches per month people make with these keywords, I suggest downloading **Publisher Rocket**. There may be a keyword closely related to the one you are researching that is far more profitable and popular. **PR** will show you this keyword, along with many other features. It is an incredibly useful tool that I also recommend, along with **KDSPY**. Don't forget to also do some research on your target audience and their wants and needs. Then finally, make a decision on the book you are going to write.

(Refer to Chapters 3, 4 & 5 for more help with this.)

(Here are shortened links for both products)

KDSPY Download >>

tinyurl.com/KDSPYlink

Publisher Rocket Download >>

tinyurl.com/procketlink

***

2 (a) - Table of Contents/Dive in! Write, Write, Write
Next, you want to create a rough table of contents for your book. Remember, this can always be changed and rearranged later as you progress. Coming up with this clearly defined structure for the book makes the writing easier and gives your book a logical progression.

It's time to transform your researched material into a book. Read other competing books in your niche and read the 3-star reviews of those books. Make it your mission to write the best book available in that niche.

Now just dive in, and move before you are ready. Develop a sense of accountability and discipline yourself to write. Setting goals and deadlines for your progress will help you finish faster and keep up the momentum. In *Chapter 1,* we spoke about why you should write a book, how it can be therapeutic, and the ideal pursuit. So, don't question yourself. Get stuck in and get the first 1000 words down.

Use everything you have learned so far in this book. Make the contents of your writing digestible and memorable. Build a connection with the reader. Use all the skills involved in story-telling and the hero's journey. You also want to build a sense of curiosity by using cliffhangers, as well as make your writing vivid by using emotional language. Finally, don't forget to keep the book simple enough for anyone to understand. If you get writer's block, go back to Chapter 9 for tips on overcoming it.

(Refer to Chapters 7, 8, & 9 for more help with this.)

2 (b) - Ghostwriter

If you choose the option of hiring a ghostwriter, you still have to do all the data research and brainstorming to find a good profitable niche. Along with this, you are going to have to write an excellent outline for your ghostwriter and a great table of contents. Do your research, and find out what competing books are missing so that your ghostwriter can focus their energy on writing your book and have a clear idea of what to do. Hiring a ghostwriter can be done on sites such as **Hotghostwriter** *(use the code* **NW101** *for a 5% discount).*

(Refer to Chapter 11 for all the details on ghostwriting.)

3 - Title

Once the book is done, you need to finalize your title. You may have done this already, and many people come up with one before writing their book but will often alter or update it afterward. The title is vitally important and can make or break your success. You need to choose something memorable, grabs attention, and resonates with your audience. Your title should instantly convey what the book is about and arouse the buyer's curiosity. You can include more keywords in your subtitle to help your book appear in searches.

(Refer to Chapter 6 for more help with this.)

4 - Finalize

Once the book is complete, it must be processed into a finished product. Start by letting the book sit for a while and then go back and edit it. Look through what you've done and make any necessary changes or add new material. Then get feedback from your friends and family. Force them to give you constructive criticism. Also, try to find people involved in the niche you've written about and ask for their feedback.

Next, you need to do deeper editing. Depending on your budget, you may want to do this yourself. Of course, you can hire a professional editor. At this point, you should also work on the layout of your book. When you're 100% pleased with your material and have read over it and updated it numerous times, it's time to commission someone to create the cover art and add illustrations - if you have any. Remember, the cover art is just as important as your title. You need to choose something that will stand out, grab attention, and sell people on buying the book. Use Fiverr to hire someone to do this for you.

Browse through their portfolios and see what you like best. Give the freelancer a good idea of what you're looking for and provide examples. It should cost no more than $10 to get a cover made. It's best to sample a couple of different freelancers. You can also ask to make the Ebook, paperback, and ACX covers for you.

5 - Description

The description part of your Amazon book is critically important, and it's something you should pay great attention to. Chapter 14 is entirely dedicated to copywriting, which is essential for advertisement. Your Amazon book page is exactly that. Use all the tricks and knowledge from this chapter to write an amazing description that will sway any customers who are unsure into purchasing your book. Then use this description on every other platform you decide to sell your book.

6 - Publishing Your Book

At last, the job is done, and it's time to share your work with the world. At this stage, you need to decide whether you're going to self-publish the book or submit it to a traditional publisher. Each of these has its advantages and disadvantages, but by now, you will have understood my advice is to self-publish. If you're going to self-publish, then you should upload your book to multiple platforms. Also, consider getting the book narrated and available for sale on Audible/ACX. Doing this will increase your sales. With Amazon being the biggest market, I suggest uploading it to KDP first and foremost. You can worry about the other platforms afterward. It's best to click the US marketplace - Amozon.com, as your primary marketplace; it is the largest by far.

Self-publishing on KDP has never been easier. The same goes for all the other platforms. Formatting the paperback will be slightly different from the Ebook size, but it's not too difficult to do, and there are plenty of great tutorials on YouTube to help you with this. From there, you can simply upload it as a Word document when it is ready to go. Be sure to preview it using the Kindle Previewer app, which is free to download.

(Refer to Chapter 12 for more help with this.)

7 - Promoting Your Book

Uploading your book to places like Amazon will eventually bring in sales, and if you use the correct SEO and find a great niche with low competition, you will have good sales. There are also a vast number of ways to promote your book online. Paid advertising such as Facebook ads, Instagram ads, and Amazon ads do not cost much and, when done right, can multiply your sales 10x. You could also consider building your own website and using marketing funnels. This will help you cut out the middleman if that's what you prefer. It's also crucial to build up some positive reviews for your book using the sites recommended in previous chapters.

(Refer to Chapters 13 & 14 for more help with this.)

Bestselling Book Ads Essentials:

Bestselling Book Ads Mastery:

As a final request (if you haven't done so already), I have a small favor to ask. As there are many similar books in this category, I have learned that gathering reviews is hugely important.

If you like what you have read and it has brought some value and knowledge to your life, it would mean a lot if you could take 30 seconds of your time and head over to amazon and write a nice brief review. A sentence or two will do.

Just scan the QR code with your phone camera and it will take you straight to the review section.

(if you are based in the UK or elsewhere, simply edit the '.com' to '.co.uk' or whatever relevant country code.)

Thank you! I can't wait to see your thoughts.

CONCLUSION

I made a promise that by the end of this book, you will have a deep understanding of what it takes to write a book and all the steps involved. You will acquire the knowledge and skills necessary to research your niche and make your book as profitable as possible. You will know how to write, market, and profit from your Ebook – and I truly hope I have achieved this.

The key thing to take away from this book is that anyone can write a book. It doesn't matter if you've never put pen to paper before (or finger to keyboard). If you can talk, tell stories, and organize your thoughts in a logical flow, then it's possible to write a book – even if you consider yourself uneducated. It's all down to self-belief and the willingness to put in an effort.

The fact is that everyone has a story that somebody out there wants to know about. Even if that isn't true, you may have a unique skill set that can help others. You could have access to secret knowledge or the answer to somebody's burning question. The bottom line is that writing books and Ebooks can be done by anybody. It doesn't matter how experienced you are or if you've never written a word in your life. You can always develop this skill.

There is also the option of ghostwriting. Once you provide a detailed outline and hire a talented ghostwriter who has knowledge in that particular topic niche, there is every chance you will have a fantastic book written for you. This allows you time to research the topic and promote your book so that you can generate good sales.

What you should understand is that books are almost entirely subjective. What one person might love, another person might hate – and vice versa. That's just the way life is. You will pick up some mediocre or negative reviews along the way, but that's part and parcel of being a writer and self-publisher. While it does matter to a certain extent, it's not absolutely crucial to be a talented writer right from the beginning. What's infinitely more important is providing value for your readers. If you write a book that provides the answers your readers are looking for, then people will be happy with your book, and you will attain positive reviews and sales. Your writing will develop as you go. You can always update your manuscripts at any time with KDP and other platforms. There is technically no right or wrong way to write a book. For every great book out there, there are many more bad books. If you implement and follow the steps given in this book, trust me, you will have done far more preparation and research than many other authors out there, and the quality and value of your book will stand out.

As we have proven, there really is a potential to make a passive income that could one day surpass your 9-5 income. If this is your goal, it is achievable with the right mindset and dedication. Becoming a writer can also bring immense amounts of joy into your life. It's therapeutic, as I've said a thousand times. And one of the best ways to spend your time. Even if you don't make a dime from your book, writing is still a great hobby. You'll look back on the period of writing as one of joy and happiness and will cherish these memories long after the book is finished. Yes, it takes a lot of hard work, but it's always worth it in the end.

I hope you take the plunge and dive into the deep end. I look forward to reading your story!

REFERENCES

Amazon.com. spend less. smile more. (n.d.). Retrieved April 12, 2022, from https://www.amazon.com/

Anderson, K. J., Penn, J., & Silvers, S. (2022, April 11). *Home.* Publisher Rocket. Retrieved April 12, 2022, from https://publisherrocket.com/

Audiobook income academy 2.0. Audiobook Income Academy. (n.d.). Retrieved April 12, 2022, from https://audiobookincomeacademy.teachable.com/p/audiobook-income-academy-2-0

Behind every review is an experience that matters. Trustpilot reviews. (n.d.). Retrieved April 12, 2022, from https://www.trustpilot.com/

BuzzFeed. (n.d.). Retrieved April 12, 2022, from https://www.buzzfeed.com/

Cameron, J. (2021). *The artists way: A spiritual path to higher creativity.* Profile Books Ltd.

Campbell, J. (2020). *The hero's journey: Joseph Campbell on his life and work.* Joseph Campbell Foundation.

Carnegie, D. (2020). *How to stop worrying and start living*. R. Sons Books.

CARNEGIE, D. A. L. E. (2022). *How to win friends and influence people*. VERMILION.

Carr, A. (2015). *Allen Carr's easy way to stop smoking*. Penguin Books.

COVEY, S. T. E. P. H. E. N. R. (2020). *7 Habits of highly effective people*. SIMON & SCHUSTER LTD.

Email marketing & more for small businesses. AWeber. (n.d.). Retrieved April 12, 2022, from https://www.aweber.com/

Ferriss, T. (2020). *The 4 hour work week: Vermilion life essentials*. Vermilion.

Fiverr - freelance services marketplace for businesses. (n.d.). Retrieved April 12, 2022, from https://www.fiverr.com/

Flesch Kincaid grade level readability test for copywriters. Perry Marshall. (n.d.). Retrieved April 12, 2022, from https://www.perrymarshall.com/grade/

Frankel, V. E. (1997). *Man's search for meaning*. Pocket Books.

Graphic resources for everyone. Freepik. (n.d.). Retrieved August 23, 2022, from https://www.freepik.com/

Greene, R., & Cent, 50. (2013). *The 50th law*. Faber & Faber.

Here are Rory's story cubes. Story Cubes. (n.d.). Retrieved April 12, 2022, from https://www.storycubes.com/en/

Home: Daily mail online. Mail Online. (n.d.). Retrieved April 12, 2022, from https://www.dailymail.com/

Kiyosaki, R. T. (2020). *Rich dad poor dad*. FBV.

Kondō Marie. (2016). *The Life-Changing Magic of Tidying up: The Japanese art of decluttering and organizing*. CreateSpace Independent Publishing Platform.

Lulu. (n.d.). Retrieved April 12, 2022, from https://www.lulu.com/

Official site to subscribe & find great reads. Reader's Digest. (2022, February 15). Retrieved April 12, 2022, from https://www.rd.com/

Pressfield, S. (2003). *The War of Art*. Orion.

Profitable book Niches & Keywords in less time. KDSPY. (n.d.). Retrieved April 12, 2022, from https://www.kdspy.com/

Quora. (n.d.). Retrieved April 12, 2022, from https://www.quora.com/

R., T. J. R., R., T. J. R., R., T. J. R., R., T. J. R., & Hammond, W. G. (2014). *The lord of the Rings.* HarperCollinsPublishers.

Self publishing | Amazon Kindle Direct Publishing. (n.d.). Retrieved April 12, 2022, from https://kdp.amazon.com/en_US/

Stay connected, informed, and inspired. Audible.com. (n.d.). Retrieved April 12, 2022, from https://www.audible.com/

The self-publisher book Ghostwriting Service. HotGhostWriter. (n.d.). Retrieved April 12, 2022, from https://hotghostwriter.com/

The world's work marketplace. Upwork. (n.d.). Retrieved April 12, 2022, from https://www.upwork.com/

Tolle, E. (2004). *The power of now: A guide to spiritual enlightenment.* Distributed to the trade by Publishers Group West.

Wikimedia Foundation. (2022, April 3). *Booktube.* Wikipedia. Retrieved April 12, 2022, from https://en.wikipedia.org/wiki/BookTube

Write your best with grammarly. Grammarly. (n.d.). Retrieved April 12, 2022, from https://www.grammarly.com/

ABOUT AUTHOR

Nicholas Woods is a freelance writer and successful entrepreneur with 12 + years of experience writing content for blogs, advertisements, and articles and ghostwriting numerous successful books across various topics. Initially working as a high school teacher with a first-class honors degree, Nicholas soon changed career paths and gained tremendous experience in digital marketing and selling online by working for top companies and writing marketing newsletters and emails. As well as being passionate about writing, Nicholas is an expert in all things related to marketing and building sustainable passive income streams. He is eager to finally share his knowledge with the world and help others do the same.

Made in the USA
Las Vegas, NV
18 September 2023